ACCELERATE

High Leverage
Leadership
for Today's
World

SUZANNE MAYO FRINDT
AND DWIGHT FRINDT

Praise for *Accelerate*
High Leverage Leadership for Today's World

The Frindts show business leaders who work in environments of pressure, stress, and fear how to live a meaningful, authentic and joyful life. This book guides so many of us to go from success to significance and to bring those we care about on the same journey.

Rafael Pastor
Chairman of the Board & CEO
Vistage International, Inc.

The book you are about to read is a remarkably simple, elegant and insightful approach to creating the possibility of consistently producing extraordinary results.

Steven H. Sunshine
Member-Management Committee
Of the International Law Firm
Of Bryan Cave LLP

The two people I know who are most committed to their brothers and sisters on the planet are Dwight and Suzanne Frindt. The evidence of their impact and reach shows up in how they relate to friends, family and their efforts to provide opportunity for those in developing countries. Their continued selfless generosity has allowed so many people around the world to live a better life. I am one of those fortunate people. This book offers you an opportunity to share their ideas and commitments as I have.

Steven J. Sherwood
CEO, CWS Capital Partners &
Chairman of the Board, The Hunger Project

Dwight and Suzanne Frindt have written a truly masterful book on leadership. This book and its' brilliant principles, clarity, accessibility, and deep wisdom are a reflection of their extensive experience and impeccable standards of excellence. But more importantly, *"Accelerate – High Leverage Leadership for Today's World"* is a complete match for the challenging times in which we live. Leaders today are facing problems and challenges that are complex beyond any previous era in history. Meeting those challenges takes extraordinary new ways of thinking and being that have been tested by the authors and made available to everyone in this absolutely stunning and brilliant book. For anyone who is truly up to something at this critical time in history—this book, *Accelerate* is a must read.

Lynne Twist
Author, The Soul of Money
Co founder, The Pachamama Alliance

The real life applications, examples, and worksheets that Dwight and Suzanne have included at the end of this book enable and empower the reader to immediately put the Operating Principles into action. For example, as a Human Resources executive, I found the information contained in "Making a Role Change" or "Closing a Performance Gap" extremely insightful and very helpful.

Kristine Carter
Vice President, Human Resources
Kawasaki Motors Corporation, U.S.A.

Simple yet profound, provocative yet practical, *Accelerate* will take you and shake you and put you back into your life and work better able and ready to BE who you were put here to be—and DO what you are capable of doing. A must-read for anyone wanting to bring their life and work together in powerful ways that transform both! What a gift! Every word exudes the substance of Dwight's and Suzanne's decades of practical experience. Much more than a "how to" book, it's a "what's real" book!

John J. Scherer
Author, Five Questions that Change Everything
Founder, The Scherer Leadership Center

A must read for those who want to increase their effectiveness muscle in collaboration and problem solving in their professional and personal lives.

Linda M. Walker
Parker Aerospace, Parker Hannifin Corporation,
Human Resources Vice President (Retired)

The fundamental principles presented in this book provide real, practical access to the kind of collaboration that will be required to deal effectively and sustainably with the fear, resistance, and unrelenting change we all face in our daily work and lives. From creating a "Yonder Star" to call you forward, to confronting your own willingness to be 100% accountable for the quality of your interactions with others, the authors provide serious readers with deceptively simple access to meaningful transformation in your work and lives.

Dr. Tom Hill
Founder of Eagle Goal Coach and
Coauthor of Chicken Soup for the
Entrepreneurial Soul

Acknowledgments

We are indebted to so many people who have influenced our thinking and the development of our work over the years and regret that we cannot enumerate each one and their unique contribution. We trust that "paying it forward" by delivering the material to our readers will serve to honor them in the way they deserve. We especially want to thank Pat Murray who first introduced us to the ideas underlying several of the Operating Principles over fifteen years ago.

Early in the game, Donna Frindt got us focused with a rigorous facilitation session to sort our myriad thoughts and ideas into a coherent outline. Kay "KC" Nash brilliantly launched us by luring us to her lovely island of Antigua for eighteen straight days of partnership in brainstorming, organizing, drafting, re-writing, re-organizing, hard work, and island fun before we had something we could call a real first draft. She and her lovable husband Willie even served us a good old USA Thanksgiving dinner during the process to keep us going. Without KC we might still be struggling to complete a coherent draft.

Steve Sunshine reviewed that draft and, with characteristic ruthless compassion, raised the bar far beyond any initial envisioning we had done. He then stuck with us through coaching emails and further rigorous editorial comments on subsequent drafts until we had satisfied his insistence that the book live up to his experience of the value of the work he has done with us over the years. What a gift!

John Gray, Tom Mullin, Bill Hunter, Linda Walker, Mike Cook, Ian Crockett, Julie Mayo, Diane Sharpe, Macy Steiner, Lee Traband, Larry Cassidy and Dale Hintz all went far beyond expectation to provide invaluable feedback on one or more of our multiple drafts over more than a year that it has taken from the time KC got us launched. Julie Mayo and Tuesday Frindt spent untold hours cutting, pasting, and retyping as we built in all of the valuable comments from these dedicated readers.

Shannon Starich started us off over 10 years ago with a number of our first graphics including the creation of our original "File Cabinet Head" figures. Christopher Nowell patiently worked with Suzanne and applied his artistic talent to our new iteration of illustrations that appear in the book.

Selina LaSalle has worked with us since the early days of 2130 Partners, and has contributed to keeping the business on track while so much time and energy has been devoted to writing the book. She is also a very dear friend as has been there for us with every kind of support imaginable during the twists and turns our business and lives have taken over the last two decades.

Kristen Clem has generously allowed her life as Suzanne's daughter to be written about, and spoken about in order to illustrate a particular point on a personal level. We especially want to thank her for allowing us to use *Suzanne's interpretation* of those events! All of our family members have played a role in shaping our thoughts and practices, so thank you to all of you who have not yet been specifically mentioned.

To conclude, we'd like to thank everyone in our lives who has had to listen to us promise "the book" or use it as an excuse for not participating in other activities for so very long.

Contents

Foreword ·xv

Prologue · xvii

Introduction ·1

Setting the Stage ·4

Unrelenting Change ·5

New Nature of Leadership—Replacing Commands
with Vision ·6

New Ways of Working Together ·7

Building Collaborative Capital Requires Upgrades · · · · · · · · · · · · · ·9

Section One–Essential Notions ·12

New Nature of Leadership–Replacing Commands with Vision · · · · 16
    Vision-Focused Leadership™ · 17
    Yonder Star–Shared Vision · 18

New Ways of Working Together · 22
    Self-Generated Accountability · 23
    Mental and Emotional Barriers–Our File Cabinet Brain · · · · · · 25
    Choice and Focus · 27
    Leadership Choice Point™ · 27

*Building Collaborative Capital Requires Relationship and
Confrontation* · 34
    Three Levels of Conversational Impact · 35
    Three Emotional Zones · 37
    Productive Dialogue · 40

Operating Principles–A Systemic Shift · 46
    Operating Principles List · 53

Contents

Section Two: It Begins with Me—Self Generated Accountability · **54**

Principle #1: Be Present, Stay in the Game ·62

Principle #2: Listen Newly, Be Intentionally Slow to Understand · · · 78

Principle #3: Take Myself Lightly ·90

Section Three: Reality Check · **104**

Principle #4: Declare There is Nothing Wrong or
Broken *Here and Now* · 110

Principle #5: Explore *truths*: Mine, Theirs and Ours · · · · · · · · · · · 128

Principle #6: Confront and Deal with Real Issues · · · · · · · · · · · · · 144

Section Four: Now Get Engaged—Productive Dialogue · · · **158**

Principle #7: Be Responsible for Creating Value · · · · · · · · · · · · · · 164

Principle #8: Make it Safe *and* Productive · · · · · · · · · · · · · · · · · · · 176

Principle #9: Be Responsible for What Gets Heard · · · · · · · · · · · · 192

Section Five: Practical Applications—Conversational Examples & Tools · **208**

Application #1: The Three Levels of Conversational
Impact as a Diagnostic Tool · 210

A Conversation About Your Conversations · · · · · · · · · · · · · · · 212

Outline · 214

Worksheet · 217

A Conversation About Your Relationship · · · · · · · · · · · · · · · · · 218

Outline · 219

Worksheet · 224

Contents

Application #2: Questions to Explore Reality—Curiosity
versus Interrogation · 226

    Example 1: A Project is Off Track · 228

    Example 2: Making a Big Decision · 231

Application #3: Eliminate the Buts! · 234

Application #4: Unmasking the Issue-Reframing "Wrong" · · · · 238

Application #5: Finding Alignment—Moving
the Conversation and the Focus "One Up" · · · · · · · · · · · · · · · 242

    Outline · 246

Application #6: Productive Delegation · · · · · · · · · · · · · · · · · · · 248

    Outline · 250

    Preparation Form · 256

Application #7: Productive Meetings · 258

    Purpose and Intended Outcomes · 262

    Worksheet · 264

Application #8: Project Performance Review · · · · · · · · · · · · · · · 266

    Outline · 269

Application #9: Dialogue for Making a Role Change or
Closing a Performance Gap · 272

    Recipe · 274

Application #10: Acknowledgement, Appreciation,
Celebration and Completion · 280

    If the Project Hasn't Been Fully Completed · · · · · · · · · · · · · · 284

Contents

Application #11: From Upset to Productivity· · · · · · · · · · · · · · · · · 286

  Shifting Your Own Upsets · 289

    Worksheet · 293

  Shifting the Upsets of Others· 295

    Worksheet · 301

Conclusion · **304**

Glossary · **307**

Index · **315**

Suggested Readings · **331**

About 2130 Partners · **335**

About the Authors· **337**

How to Reach Us—For More Support · · · · · · · · · · · · · · · · · · · **339**

Foreword

All leaders are engaged in the same valiant and sacred quest. That quest has been dissected and analyzed in thousands of books claiming to have discovered the "secret" solution. The quest, of course, is to produce meaningful results, results that inspire, that produce tangible rewards, that create loyalty and provide inspiration.

Producing results, any results, is the exception, not the rule. From the latest three-year strategic plan to the newest reorganization, as leaders we search for ways to cause something (anything?) to happen. This search is littered with the unsuccessful new approaches which sprout up every two or three years. This graveyard of new approaches is a "buzzword" lover's delight…from TQM to the obligatory mission statement. These approaches tend to focus in one particular direction…how might we get others to do what they need to do?

The book you are about to read travels in a different direction and is a remarkably simple, elegant, and insightful approach to creating the possibility of consistently producing extraordinary results. It builds on the simple premise that while we often focus on others and their roles in producing (or not producing) results, in fact, producing results is all about us, the leaders. Our perceptions, our interactions, and our approaches are in fact all we can control and, as it turns out, are all we need.

Steven H. Sunshine
Member-Management Committee
Of the International Law Firm
Of Bryan Cave LLP

Prologue

What Started Us on the Path That Has Led to Writing This Book?

Dwight:

Two things profoundly changed the course of my life and my perception of how extraordinary results are produced.

In 1977 my life path was permanently altered when I attended a presentation of a new idea, a commitment to the end of hunger on the planet called The Hunger Project. At that time, the idea of *ending* hunger was beyond impossible. Its bold approach was a quantum leap from the prevailing context of despair and resignation surrounding the existing world agreement that hunger couldn't be ended. It suggested a radically different approach–transform thinking about the condition itself. The Hunger Project stared into the persistence of hunger across the globe and took a whole new look at the relevance of the then prevailing actions being taken by the world's institutions and people. The Hunger Project demanded that we intervene in and stand for shifting humanity's prevailing paradigm from "it can't be done" to "it will be done."

It took about a year for the idea of creating a new context or paradigm to transform the way I thought about and experienced life. I had three young daughters and often found myself worrying about the world in which they and their kids would grow up and wondering how I could use my life to positively impact the outcome. I lived very near "ground zero" of a Trident nuclear submarine base, which meant that any serious break in the détente between the United States and the Soviet Union could result in that initial "push of the button" that would land a round of deadly missiles close enough to wipe us out within about ten minutes of launch. While I could not imagine at the time how I could impact that global threat, The Hunger Project offered me direct action to impact the global issue of hunger and poverty. In my mind, that result could ease East-West tension, and my family and all families would have a safer, healthier world to live in. I embraced the idea that participating with The Hunger Project was a real opportunity for leadership in altering the way the world was headed.

The opportunity to work at the cutting edge of causing such a shift was so compelling that I left my chief operating officer role and made a commitment that led to spending two years of my life as a full-time volunteer for The Hunger Project. The idea of transforming my frame of reference and taking actions that had the biggest reach and impact I could imagine began to be a new way of sorting priorities for me. My commitment to work at the core of issues and to widely share the opportunity to apply that methodology of shifting context to produce unprecedented outcomes in any area of life has been broadening and deepening for me ever since.

The second defining moment came nearly a decade later when I learned that my wife, Shannon, had lost her life when her car was run off the road by a drunk driver. Over the next months I experienced a very dark time. I really had to search for what matters in life. The finality of the situation left me with little interest in relationships of any kind, whether personal or business, where quality is traded off for safety, the status quo, and avoiding what's not working. I became devoted to what matters and what works in communicating with others. Being complete with each person every time we met became essential, as I learned that any such meeting could be our last. I have become intensely focused on the availability of love, effective communication, and producing meaningful results with and for each and every person with whom I interact.

From The Hunger Project I have distilled that focusing on shifting the context, or paradigm, in which we consider both the issues we face and the relationships in which we are engaged is the methodology that enables unprecedented outcomes. Shannon's death brought home that now, or the present, is the only time we have to make that happen.

Suzanne:

In my early thirties I experienced some dramatic wake-up calls that set me on a path of personal and leadership development. For a period of twelve years early in my career, I worked for a fast-growing entrepreneurial firm where I was challenged continually to contribute and grow. Though there were promotions for me during that time, a theme ran through my annual performance evaluations: "learn to get along with others"; "work on your communication"; "soften your approach." During my sixth-year performance appraisal, my boss once again praised the goals I had accomplished. This time he added: "Suzanne, we may have to let you go. While we are pleased to have the great financial results, we can no longer afford the fallout that occurs around you. To continue to grow our company, it will require having leaders who can produce results with teams of people. Around you there is way too much turnover and damage control required. Unless you take that on seriously and shift the way you operate, we will have to let you go." I was in shock. Up until then I had been very righteous about the best way to communicate—very directly and with "honesty," which often occurred to others as needlessly brutal and harsh.

During the same time frame I was finalizing my divorce after twelve years of marriage. When a conversation would turn into an argument in my marriage, we could not deal with it in any effective way. We hadn't developed any conversational muscle to work through tough issues together successfully. My limited life skills left me with little ability to work through issues with my husband. The only tool in my bag was to avoid confronting issues. Whenever a tough topic came up that might threaten "marital peace," I would mentally and emotionally make it off limits. Often I would tell myself that it wasn't that big of a deal or it wasn't worth risking the relationship to "go there." Over time we couldn't (or didn't dare) talk about money, politics, my job, my boss, or even about having another child. Eventually there wasn't anything that was really important to me that we could talk about, and I am sure the same was true for my husband. At the time, I just didn't know how to raise and resolve issues productively and still maintain, let alone enrich, my relationships. I didn't raise them at home for fear of losing the relationship, and I raised them boldly and unproductively at work, considering the results more important than the relationships.

Ultimately, with a failed marriage and a stalled career, I faced up to my limited skills. I used both situations as a wake-up call and took a hard and painful look at my behaviors and limiting beliefs about communication and relationships. The focus of my work ever since has been building collaborative skills, learning to work through issues, and finding ways to strengthen relationships.

Our paths join...

We became colleagues in the mid-1980s and marriage partners in 1991. As we explored what a shared purpose might be for our marriage, we chose to dedicate our lives and relationship to influencing resources and resourcefulness such that each and every person on the planet has the opportunity for a healthy and productive life. This commitment has led to significant deepening of our involvement with The Hunger Project (www.thp.org) and to the formation of our leadership development and education firm, 2130 Partners (www.2130partners.com). To further increase our reach and impact, we became Chairs for Vistage International, Inc. (www.vistage.com), and Suzanne added international speaking to her activities. Most recently we have added a new dimension to the context in which we live our lives by becoming investors in The Pachamama Alliance (www.pachamama.org). This strategic, transformational movement is addressing the critical importance of awakening ourselves to a new relationship with each other and our earth if we are to leave an environmentally sustainable, spiritually fulfilling, and socially just legacy for coming generations.

The actions we take in our lives are informed and guided by the overarching commitment we have created for ourselves. We are constantly on the lookout for opportunities to extend the reach and impact of our resources, our work, and ourselves on behalf of that commitment.

This book...

Our work with The Hunger Project has had a profound influence on development of the contextual material in this book, particularly Vision-Focused Leadership and the Leadership Choice Point.

In 2130 Partners' early days, we focused our work on what we called Strategic Intent, a declaration describing vision, mission, values, and bold goals. While our clients were relatively successful in designing these declarations for themselves, we were bothered by the lack of consistent progress they seemed to make relative to the boldness of their declarations. In examining the patterns, we realized that the shortfalls in delivering on the promise of the Strategic Intent work seemed to start almost immediately, occurred in daily action, and were not really identified as causal factors. Our constant inquiry into what was missing, or present and acting as a roadblock that, if addressed would dramatically increase leadership effectiveness, has led us to the formulation and assembly of the material and methodologies in this book.

Enjoy.

Introduction

ACCELERATE

HIGH LEVERAGE LEADERSHIP
FOR TODAY'S WORLD

Our first intention in writing this book is for you to become able to sustainably expand your reach and impact and that of the people around you, whether individually, in your work in teams, or in your personal lives, to levels you never thought possible.

We have no idea what the ideal level is for you. That is rightfully your concern and, by the way, we are confident that there is no right answer, other than yours. Our own vision for our reach and impact has grown to be 25,000 miles, the world around, and seven generations. Two of our longest, dearest friends are, on the other hand, fully expressed in their lives, mostly within the city limits of Corona Del Mar, California. The extreme difference in focus has no bearing on the quality of our relationship.

Our view is that there is an intention that wants to use your life, a self-expression that's dying to get out, and that it's your job to reveal it and live it as fully as you can for the rest of your life. Make it the core element of your life's work.

Our second intention for the book is that you become able and use the opportunity to access a whole new level of self-expression in your interactions with others and theirs with you. If this calls to you, take on the principles and methodologies with a vengeance. Life will become so much more meaningful and satisfying than you can now imagine.

Our third intention is that you and those around you increase your collaborative skills and thereby your creativity, agility, and effectiveness to the levels that will be required for leadership in our world of unrelenting change. Your new ability to be present to the facts and data about the world around you, to address fear directly, and to move through resistance, whether your own or from others, will cause your performance to jump to the level required to be extraordinarily successful and grow rapidly from there.

Our fourth intention is that you be well. We have long questioned behaviors, whether economic, political, or personal, that diminish the soul's expression. We expect that the new freedom you will find as you begin to own the mental models and Operating Principles offered here will unleash you. The newfound peace that goes with that can, in turn, express itself in a healthier body and lifestyle, healthier relationships with your co-workers, and healthier relationships throughout your family and community life.

Given our commitment to reach and impact, we intend that, as you and others adopt and practice this material in your own lives, the new way of living that evolves will spread far and wide and will eventually allow human beings to find new ways to relate and live peacefully and sustainably across our earth. We invite you to join us in adding this commitment to your way of being as you lead your life at new, high levels of effectiveness, productivity, contribution, and satisfaction.

Suzanne & Dwight Frindt

Setting the Stage

Unrelenting Change

Our world is rapidly reshaping in many amazing ways:

- As the video *Shift Happens* has pointed out to the millions of YouTube viewers who have seen it on the Internet, "We are currently preparing students for jobs that don't exist, who will be using technology we haven't yet discovered, to solve problems we don't even yet know about yet" (*Shift Happens* video, created by Karl Fisch and modified by Scott McLeod).

- The quantity of information and its availability and speed of delivery are increasing at an exponential rate as costs are approaching zero.

- The number of people accessing and using this information and the many ways it is disseminated has exploded since the advent of personal computers and the Internet—which in turn exponentially speeds up the rate at which new technologies are developed.

- Women are stepping into leadership roles at all levels, in diverse venues and in unprecedented numbers all over the world.

- Awareness that our global environment cannot continue to withstand a collective human consumption race is spreading quickly.

- Our children are being born into and growing up in a world so different than the one we grew up in that it requires a new way of being for them to lead successful lives.

- More people over 65 are alive today than have ever lived to that age, so that group will be looking for whole new models for leading healthy, successful lives.

New Nature of Leadership—Replacing Commands with Vision

In this evolving new reality, successful leadership will have a very different nature than traditional approaches.

It was quite different to be a leader in simpler economic times and when the world moved at a slower pace with less connectivity. There were successful models and practices in place as well as more easily identifiable and attainable goals. Patterns of entitlement offered at least the illusion of security, and there was more time and predictability in producing results. However, now—when previous business models and assumptions have been turned on their heads, when people's livelihoods are changing and disappearing regularly, and when successful businesses are being transformed for the new realities—the leadership required is radically agile, proactive, and creative.

Leaders who will be effective in this time of incredible opportunity are those that lead as if they are in a dance with reality—that is, they look to create exciting new paradigms, processes, and even companies based on creating the next game while being responsible for the current and unfolding global economy. They are not simply waiting until the economy gets back to normal or using past experiences to map out current pathways.

Being in a dance demands conversations appropriate to dancing. Think about it—when you get out on the dance floor, do you tell your partner, "I need these four steps from you in the next minute, followed by a repetitive pattern until I tell you otherwise"? If you have done that, perhaps you have found that it leaves you with very few dance partners. How then do you engage with others in this new reality?

New Ways of Working Together

As we go forward, those who lead will be the ones taking advantage of the creativity and productivity gains available by focusing on the human, collaborative dimension, while laggards will suffer in the face of unrelenting change.

The extremely affordable and nearly instant access to vast amounts of information and ways of interacting with whole communities that are becoming available, combined with a productive attitude toward change and the new realities it brings, creates huge opportunities for you and your leadership. However, leading *effectively* will require a new mind-set to unleash potential and creativity and to capitalize on opportunities.

The challenges lie in strengthening your ability to choose the direction, form the goals, and then communicate and enroll others so that you build groups and organizations that can collectively navigate shifting realities. This means improving your ability to communicate, work together collaboratively, and lead others to do so as well. If you learn how to identify and utilize the navigational guides to traversing this uncharted territory, you will experience higher productivity, more rapid innovation, and greater organizational agility. Additionally, responsiveness to the needs of customers and other stakeholders in the organization and more rewarding relationships will become something you can rely upon.

The new array of technologies gives you ways to connect to information and to each other via machines, yet can lessen your need to connect on a personal basis. As a result of personal digital assistants (PDAs), voice mail, and Internet access around the globe, you can receive and transmit messages without ever hearing a live voice or seeing a live face. This constant dealing in cyberspace can easily result in social isolation, where interpersonal and collaborative skills are relegated to the sidelines or, even worse, begin to disappear.

Daniel Goleman, in his book *Social Intelligence,* talks about "creeping disconnection" that has produced a two-decade decline in social capital. In a survey of 4,830 people in the United States, he found that for many, the Internet has replaced television as the way free time is used. For every hour people spent using the Internet, their face-to-face contact with friends, co-workers, and family fell by twenty-four minutes. He further comments, "To the extent that technology absorbs people in a virtual reality, it deadens them to those who are actually nearby."

This personal isolation, combined with the increasing rate of change and immediacy of deadlines, has exacerbated an already challenged workplace where people have difficulty working through often relatively simple situations with each other. An inordinate amount of productive time, payroll dollars, and opportunities are lost daily, monthly, and annually to the distraction caused by unresolved or nonproductive interactions. In today's world, if a company saw the same kind of losses in a manufacturing or supply process, it would be forced to quickly shut down and retool or risk becoming another in the growing list of "has-been brands."

When asking our executive clients a simple question, "What time could you go home if everyone in the company simply came to work, did their jobs and went home?" the answer used to surprise us until it kept being repeated. On average, our clients say, "Between 10:30 and 11:00 a.m."

If so many executives perceive that they could go home before lunch (or get twice as much work done every day) if everyone just showed up, did their work, and went home, what's taking up so much of their time? Our clients tell us it is dealing with all the upsets, push-back, miscommunications, broken promises, failed intentions, and frustrations with their interactions. They feel that one of the most time-consuming parts of their job is managing distressed interactions—between their team members and with customers and vendors—so that the important work actually gets done, promises are kept, the organization's values are honored, and the business stays on its strategic course. While not necessarily new, the pace of unrelenting change and the constant media hype around economic and global uncertainties have exacerbated this issue. This whole mess of friction and waste that occurs in an organization's daily communications produces high levels of stress and its associated health risks and makes work incredibly inefficient.

Let's assume there's exaggeration at play here. Even if you will never be able to consistently leave by noon or double your effectiveness, it is entirely reasonable to gain at least two hours of your time every day through minimizing dealing with distress in yourself and your team members. That's nearly five hundred extra hours a year that can be devoted to creative thinking, visioning, and strategizing rather than on repairing, to say nothing at this point about the increase in morale and well-being. That amounts to substantial savings—and the same can be said for everyone throughout the organization. It's clear that a dramatic increase in a team's productivity is available through getting much, much better at communicating and working collaboratively. Just as lean manufacturing and supply chain compression have increased competitiveness and lowered cost by eliminating waste in processes, leaders and leading firms will be taking advantage of these human dimension gains in productivity and laggards will suffer as we go forward in these unprecedented times.

Building Collaborative Capital Requires Upgrades

To effectively change our outer reality requires being willing to shift our inner reality.

Today, talented, educated people who know how and are motivated to work interactively with each other are the key to success for more and more businesses. This new collaborative approach means many more minds are put to work on the opportunities and challenges facing us whether in business, in our organizations, or even in our families.

When we were born we came equipped with the most powerful computers on earth (although *Shift Happens* cites projections that the quantitative computing power of a supercomputer will pass that of the human brain by the year 2013). These innate computers serve us well in producing new ideas and dynamic solutions—as we can see in all that has happened just in the past twenty years of technological growth. The core thought processes that guide our reactions and interactions were mostly loaded into your brain and ours when we were children and have been chugging along ever since, functioning as an unconscious and unexamined operating system.

Don't change the world, change worlds...starting with your own.

Adapted from **St. Francis of Assisi–**
Catholic patron saint of animals and the environment

Being able to think in new ways requires challenging the very basis of your own thinking—your self-concept, worldview, and automatic ways of interacting with others. The methodologies offered in this book allow you to intervene in your historic mental operating system so you can displace many of your own unexamined, unproductive thought and behavior patterns with effective ways to think and interact. These interventions, or upgrades will give you the skills to have authentic conversations and relationships and be more creative in your thinking about virtually every business and personal situation you encounter. Then you can model and foster engagement and collaboration with those around you.

The operating system upgrades presented in this book are based on decades of work with our clients, interactions with hundreds of other speakers and writers, and our own studies. Using them, we have increased our own effectiveness and satisfaction, as have many of our clients and course participants. We describe the basis of these upgrades as **Essential Notions** and **Operating Principles.**

Section One:
Essential Notions

Before you begin redesigning your thinking and interactions from the Operating Principles presented in this book, it is essential to understand some of our foundational concepts and terms. These Essential Notions provide the context for applying the Operating Principles and for the new leadership practices you will be able to develop. To use a construction analogy: consider the old paradigm of command and control leadership as a building foundation. Over time, leadership and management practices and communication styles have been built on that foundation to accommodate and fit in with the initial foundation design. In most cases, as with the foundation of most buildings, the foundation itself is no longer visible. To build new leadership and management practices for the emerging new world, it would be insufficient to leave the foundational structure and simply replace the walls, windows and roof. New practices that work will not fit on top of an obsolescing foundation. The old foundation will most likely cause the practices to be reshaped to fit the old design. Reframing your thinking and conversations through application of the Operating Principles is similar to designing and constructing a new foundation for your new building. The building then represents the new leadership thinking, communication structures, and behaviors appropriate to the new world and its reshaped marketplaces.

Our phrasing and the way we use terms in this text are not designed to be conventional or necessarily grammatically correct. Our selections are based on our experience of what works—on what plays out powerfully in the action when our clients and students engage with the language and each other. If we find ideas and ways of expressing them that produce and advance something new and interesting, we are excited. If we just see more of the same old types of interactions, then bye-bye terminology! Consequently, we have revised our terminology and our individual principles over time, adding and subtracting as we have gone along.

The Essential Notions

New Nature of Leadership—Replacing Commands with Vision

Vision-Focused Leadership™

Yonder Star–Shared Vision

New Ways of Working Together

Self-Generated Accountability

Mental and Emotional Barriers—Our File Cabinet Brain

Choice and Focus

Leadership Choice Point™

Building Collaborative Capital Requires Relationship and Confrontation

Three Levels of Conversational Impact

Three Emotional Zones

Productive Dialogue

Operating Principles–A Systemic Shift

Operating Principles

New Nature of Leadership— Replacing Commands with Vision

Vision-Focused Leadership™

We call the management model we use to replace the old "command-and-control" paradigm **Vision-Focused Leadership,** which is an approach grounded in shared vision and built through collaboration. When we first started talking about this foundational shift in our thought process, it was fairly novel in the business world. This process of developing plans based on a shared vision has become more accepted. Its success in facilitating cultures that can adapt quickly and creatively to changing conditions has made it attractive for businesses and leaders committed to thriving in uncertainty. A still unique characteristic of how we use Vision-Focused Leadership with clients, however, is our focus on the design of the particular human interactions necessary to effectively and sustainably fulfill vision. The material in this book has been created to allow you to increase your ability to have those types of interactions, whether you are working with a whole team to fulfill an overall corporate strategic vision or simply sharing a vision for a great relationship with a special person in your life.

Vision: A mental image produced by the imagination

Vision-Focused Leadership as a mental model shows how thinking, listening, speaking, and actions—most importantly those that you employ to lead others—are focused and informed by a shared vision. Focusing on your shared vision allows you to make choices; orient your creativity, energy, and resources; and correlate your thoughts and actions and the actions of people working with you on your shared intention. In the absence of shared vision, it is easy to become victims of or be distracted by circumstances, worries, and fears, and to react based on instant, automatic, unconscious, and unexamined thoughts, beliefs, and judgments stored in your mind. Without necessarily realizing it, the past winds up driving your bus.

> When we talk about leadership here, our intention is to stress that leadership can be evoked anywhere in an organization—that is, every person can exhibit leadership qualities, no matter what his or her job description may be.

There has been much experimental research in the field of social psychology to demonstrate the benefits of a "shared social identity" as a precursor to team development and effectiveness. The process of developing a shared vision and working toward fulfillment creates an opportunity for powerful shared social identity—a deep feeling of "us." In addition to benefiting from a shared vision as a navigational beacon (a contextual and directional icon) it also serves as the social glue that binds a group together. This is critical for our work together since, in today's world, we are forming groups that are more and more diverse in geography, language, background, and life experience. The homogeneity or sameness that once held groups together can also lead to being insular, exclusive, or narrow minded and can limit possibilities without your awareness.

If you and your team members have done a good job developing and sharing the vision, then creating powerful actions will flow much more naturally. People will be able to individually source their ideas, actions, and interactions from the shared vision. If you replace commands with shared vision and broaden the *source and responsibility* for creativity to the entire team, you will maximize creativity, ownership, collaboration, and velocity in fulfilling the shared vision.

Yonder Star–Shared Vision

We use the term **Yonder Star** to include shared vision, goals, objectives, and strategies to obtain it. It can be applied at any level from a strategic corporate vision to your vision for the outcomes you intend to produce in a single conversation or meeting. The Yonder Star is the ideal, *out* in front of you and *up* above the path you are currently traveling, that provides a common focus and inspires your actions. Rather than hanging onto sacred past-based activities and processes (e.g., "what did we do and how did we do it last year?"), priorities, plans, and milestones are designed from a focus on the Yonder Star. From this mind-set, actions are prioritized by their value in fulfilling the Yonder Star. All members of the team are inspired to explore their own integration of the goal with their passion to contribute and the specific role their work will play in its fulfillment. From shared dedication to the overall outcome, a pervasive attitude of "I've got your back" naturally develops within each member of the team. Dissent, one-upmanship, and agendas fueled by self-interest tend to fade to the background.

Vision-Focused Leadership

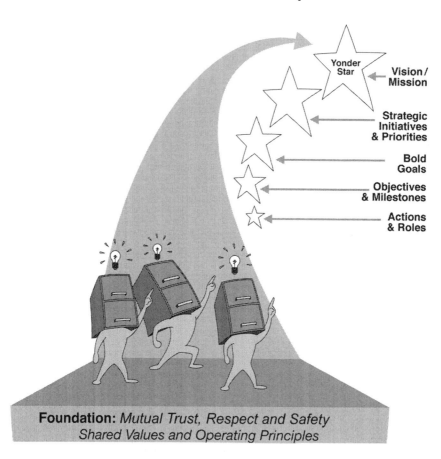

Yonder Star — Vision / Mission

Strategic Initiatives & Priorities

Bold Goals

Objectives & Milestones

Actions & Roles

Foundation: *Mutual Trust, Respect and Safety*
Shared Values and Operating Principles

The graphic at the left is our shorthand illustration of this notion. Here we show a group of people who are interacting from a solid foundation of mutual trust, respect, and safety to reach their mutual Yonder Star. In this case, a collection of aligned Yonder Stars, shown in a stack of different sizes, depicts the many intermediate goals that lie between your current situation and fulfillment of your Yonder Star. To sort out which actions will be most productive on your route to your Yonder Star, look back from your fulfilled Yonder Star and ask, "What's missing in our current reality that, if we work on it, will accelerate fulfilling our Yonder Star?" From your list, determine the decisions and actions that will be most leveraged in closing the gap. By *leveraged*, we mean the actions that produce the greatest impact while requiring the fewest resources and taking the least amount of time to accomplish. Get started, monitor results, recalibrate with new position updates, and continue on your path or make adjustments as necessary to stay on course.

◇◇◇

He turns not back who is bound to a star.

Leonardo da Vinci–*Italian Painter, Sculptor, Architect, Inventor and Scientist*

◇◇◇

In the Productive Dialogues discussion in this book, we will suggest how to move your interactions and conversations "up and out," continuously resourcing and reconnecting at least one level up from the current situation to create better solutions or resolve issues more effectively. Be sure to check out the recommendations and outline in the Practical Application—Section Five: *Finding Alignment—Moving the Conversation and the Focus "One Up"*.

New Ways of Working Together

Self-Generated Accountability

One of the differentiators of the material in this book is the emphasis on personal responsibility.

When leaders and managers tell us that they would like to be able to hold their people more accountable, we often hear that they would really like them to be "obedient," follow the orders or instructions, *and* be willing to take the blame if things don't work out. The whole concept of buy-in or shared ownership is missing. Inside a command and control environment, buy-in and ownership have been twisted to be something "required."

In Dr. Stanley Milgram's controversial and infamous experiments in the early sixties exploring obedience and responsibility, the Yale University professor conducted an experiment using residents of New Haven, Connecticut, and actors. The stated research objective was to determine whether learning is enhanced with the administration of pain through increasing electric shock. The real purpose of the study was to determine how willing ordinary people were to replace personal responsibility with obedience to (scientific) authority. When told to do so by the scientific researchers, 65% of the subjects were willing to give apparently harmful electric shocks to the "learners" (actors) who were pitifully protesting further shocks, in spite of the fact that the victims did nothing to "deserve" that level of punishment except give incorrect answers. Later, Jerry Burger at Santa Clarita University in California conducted a partial replication of Milgram's famous studies, which was featured in the January 3, 2007 broadcast of ABC News' *Primetime*. Burger's work on social influence and compliance showed similar results. What was different about the participants who stopped administering the shocks? In interviews of participants after the experiments, as reported in the *New York Times*, "Those who stopped generally believed themselves to be responsible for the shocks, whereas those who kept going tended to hold the experimenter accountable."

Consider the experiment's implications on your understanding and use of the concept of accountability. When individuals see themselves as the source of responsibility for their actions, their ownership of the project or task informs their actions in a productive way. When individuals believe someone else is responsible, they follow instructions without engaging their own thought processes and discernment. It doesn't really matter whether you tell them that you are "holding them accountable" or not. The shift only occurs with their choice of perspective. Which set of behaviors do you intend to foster in your team or in your organization?

To foster Self-Generated Accountability, a new model of leadership that replaces commands with vision and a collaborative culture is required. While some leaders and managers may, at times, simply desire obedience, the trade-off they make is to lose any natural Self-Generated Accountability from those doing the work. In response to an environment requiring obedience masquerading as accountability, people who would normally thrive in a true accountability culture eventually leave, and you are left with those who simply want to be told what to do. Then, if the plan fails, they are off the hook since they were "just doing what they were told." We call this "vicious obedience" or "malicious compliance"—a far cry from accountability. We discuss the Operating Principles that will guide you in upgrading your own mental operating system to this orientation in Section Two of this book, "It Begins with Me."

What Gets in Our Way?
Mental and Emotional Barriers—Our File Cabinet Brain

Your individual and unique brain is the storehouse for your lifelong memories, experiences, emotions, judgments, and beliefs that you access instantly and automatically to compare, assess, and process all current incoming data and experiences. We use the metaphor of a **File Cabinet** to symbolize the way minds operate like a filing system to perceive, filter, file, retrieve, and use input.

The characters with the file cabinets for heads in the prior Yonder Star illustration that are all pointing to the Yonder Star graphically represents the way each of us draws on our mental File Cabinet, even when we are engaged in pursuit of a shared Yonder Star. In this case, the participants are sharing their ideas and experiences with an intention to contribute productively toward achieving the shared vision. In this mode, new ideas and solutions can emerge from outside any individual member of the group's File Cabinet mind. They flow from and are a function of the collaborative interaction by the participants.

In this next illustration the File Cabinet characters demonstrate how we often use our past-based knowledge and beliefs to engage unproductively with fellow team members. Here they are busy spewing their own File Cabinet contents; opinions, perspectives, judgments and experiences out into the interaction in "convince and convert" mode without any regard for the other person or what they may have to contribute. These characters have lost focus on the Yonder Star and are turning energy, creativity, and wits to winning the battle over who is right. Defense kicks in and the challenge is on. The best possible outcome, after a challenge between individuals based only on past-based experiences, is that *one* perspective will prevail, usually the person with the most power in the relationship. Once the volume or intensity of a dueling File Cabinet discussion gets turned up, unproductive emotions are often triggered on both sides, diminishing or destroying the opportunity for an environment of productivity, creativity, buy-in and ownership. Often the most elegant solution does not exist in either File Cabinet. It is sparked and developed through sharing and developing creative ideas, thoughts, and experiences.

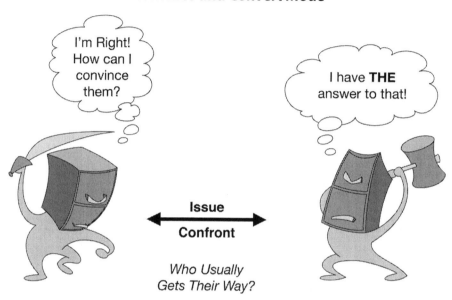

Dueling File Cabinets
Convince and Convert Mode

Throughout this book, we will explore mental and emotional barriers that can arise from your own File Cabinet to keep you from being present and making choices consistent with your Yonder Star. We will offer solutions for observing and disengaging or untangling yourself from some of the traps associated with those barriers so you can be open to new ideas and new ways of interacting. During those discussions, you may find yourself focusing on how you can fix your business associates, relatives, and friends with the ideas. Remember: give that up. The material is for *you* to practice, practice, and practice some more.

Choice and Focus

We think we live in the world. We think we live in a set of circumstances, but we don't. We live in our conversations about the world and our conversations about the circumstances. When we're in a conversation about fear…then that is the world we inhabit. If we're in a conversation about possibility…then that is the world we inhabit.

Lynne Twist–*The Soul of Money*

Leadership Choice Point™

There are many unconscious and compelling influences on your actions in each moment. Your subconscious mind is always busy monitoring and reacting to your circumstances, comparing the incoming data to your past, checking for threats to your survival, and using your past as a basis to anticipate and control what may happen in the next moment. Meanwhile, other parts of your mind are busy checking for your emotions and your storehouse of possibly relevant concepts. If you are truly conscious and present in the moment, you can choose to access your Yonder Star and use it to guide your decisions, conversations, and actions (illustrated by the upper line in the graphic on the next page). When it sinks in that you really do have a choice in each moment, you will become able to regularly re-choose how to be, how to interact, and what to do next to reach your goals. The power and leverage in this idea is that you can think newly and reelect the source of your next thoughts and actions—The Leadership Choice Point!

The paragraphs that follow describe the impact of correlating our thoughts and actions with each of the three focal points illustrated in our Leadership Choice Point graphic: Vision/Yonder Star, Circumstances, or Fears.

Leadership Choice Point

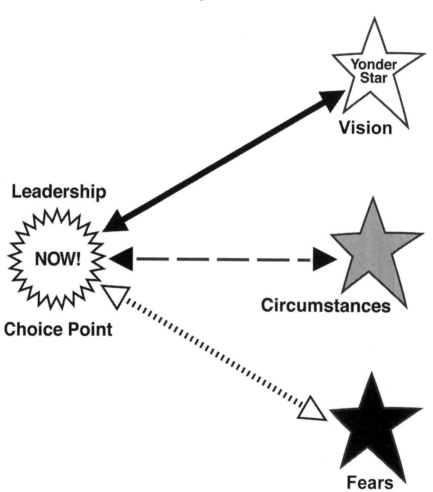

Fear-Based Focus

When fear is in charge, you are reacting to a real or perceived threat. Your brain compares incoming data with records in your File Cabinet and issues instantaneous survival commands, which severely limit your conscious thinking, and focuses your behaviors in a defensive mode. You are in *reaction* mode versus *choice* mode. Your reactions become limited to fight, flight, freeze, or appease, depending on your particular survival technique. Analysis, options, and perspectives are not available as your focus narrows and becomes limited to your survival. Productive connections with others are pretty much nonexistent.

A focus on our fears, worries, and concerns, this mode of thought, and the manner of listening and speaking that results, is represented along the lower line in the illustration. Since this reaction is instant and automatic, it is often unrecognized. You may be spending much more time in a very low-effectiveness, fear-based interaction mode than you realize.

Under the Circumstances

Without even realizing it, most of the day you are automatically correlating your actions with your circumstances. One of the characteristics of circumstances is that they are fairly predictable, with some exceptions such as a vacation in a foreign country or a new job. Most of your day is filled with common activities, such as walking, driving, sitting in chairs, eating meals, engaging with others, and so on. Most of the time your brain can count on what will be required in the next moment because the majority of the incoming data matches the historical records in your File Cabinet—so it knows the signals to send to successfully negotiate the current circumstances. You may drive safely down the road for extended periods, often without being consciously aware, because your brain recognizes the physical circumstances and knows the rules to apply as it issues commands to your muscles. Probably you have wondered, at least once, whether you stopped at that last stop sign or not. Fortunately, you didn't have to consciously think about it. Your brain works hard to match the current moment with the past even when the fit may be relatively poor, and then directs your actions in a manner consistent with that interpretation.

———◇◇◇———

Whenever you think that you are facing a contradiction, examine your premises.

John Galt in *Atlas Shrugged*, **Ayn Rand**

———◇◇◇———

Unconsciously correlating your actions with your circumstances doesn't always work! When you are no longer able to produce outcomes that are desirable or advantageous or the circumstances are suddenly unrecognizable, it is time to face the fact that you may be hanging on to predictable, past-based notions and behaviors that don't apply or aren't productive now!

Unconsciously allowing circumstances to govern your actions is not the only unproductive maneuver. Some of our clients have justified *conscious* correlation of their actions with their circumstances by calling that behavior "being realistic" or "living in the real world." Their wording may even include "under the circumstances." When an individual or team insists that the circumstances they are facing are the defining boundaries and limitations of their thinking, they are truly "under the circumstances."

Most people live a circumstantial life

This conscious acceptance of current conditions as the limiting conditions is a setup for victimhood—being a victim of the circumstances. In day-to-day conversations it often shows up as a limiting belief such as "You know how Sally is…" which turns the "way they are" into a reality—a current condition that limits options and possibilities. If you are really good at these consciously created limitations, you will find proof, evidence, and collusion from others that the circumstances as you see them are right and that you are a victim of them—nothing can be done "under the circumstances." David Whyte talks about a "Contingency Life": as soon as all the circumstances can be arranged perfectly, then I can…"get a job"…"go back to school"… "have a great relationship."

Yonder Star Focus

Reactions based on fear and automatic behavior correlated with your circumstances are driven mostly from a subconscious level. While a focus on your Yonder Star requires conscious choice, it may also bring up a certain amount of fear for you or others. Yonder Stars, as we define them, are new creations, have less evidence or track record for support, and involve outcomes that can't simply be predicted from past successes. The unknown associated with this perspective can evoke doubts, which turn into fears quite readily.

The essential self-management skill here is to intervene in your own thinking and behavior and act from the Leadership Choice Point. In each Leadership Choice Point moment, you will be making a conscious and courageous intervention in your own thinking and behaviors to realign them with your goals. Perhaps the greater of these two is courage, as it is basically a way of being. The conscious mind is geared to sorting concepts and may not give you access to the "juice" you must summon to trust your "gut feel" or "instinct" at critical moments. It is only in repeatedly re-choosing your Yonder Star, in the present moment, over fear or known circumstances that new pathways to your desired outcomes can emerge and you can develop the capacity to be comfortable with higher levels of uncertainty and unfamiliarity.

> *David Whyte, poet and author, defines courage as: cultivating a healthy relationship with the unknown.*

We are not saying that correlating your actions with fear or circumstances is bad or wrong. Each can be useful at appropriate moments. The key takeaway here is to learn to be aware that you have a choice in each moment so that you are refreshing yourself in a way that your thoughts and actions are more creative, powerful, and collaborative. Your ability to be present and consider choices versus operating on cruise control will greatly impact your success. The Operating Principles are designed to help you do just that.

We have not yet seen anyone (including ourselves or among our numerous clients) who is able to remain focused and operating on the upper line at all times. There is nothing wrong with having your attention on circumstances or being afraid. In a normal situation, you will often have all three focuses occurring in rapid succession within a short period! In one moment, you are focused on your Yonder Star. Then you realize the *huge* gap between your vision and the present reality, start to worry, and *bam*, you're on the lower line. You catch yourself and work on getting "realistic," which generally means focusing on your circumstances. That action can then drive you right back down the lower line. Alternatively, you might deceive yourself into thinking the current circumstances will go on forever and get comfortable, pretending to be present. Then you remember what you are committed to and choose the Yonder Star path again.

The objective is not to keep an unblinking focus on your Yonder Star. Learn how to catch yourself, identify where you really are focused in the moment, and refocus. The payoff is less emotional and mental downtime and less friction and waste in your conversations and relationships. Learning to consciously choose in this way more frequently is an outcome of the paradigm shift to Vision-Focused Leadership and an essential ingredient of Self-Generated Accountability.

Building Collaborative Capital Requires Relationship *and* Confrontation

Every intention is moved forward or threatened by every conversation.

Three Levels of Conversational Impact

Whenever we connect face-to-face or voice-to-voice, our brains for all practical purposes interlock. Each interaction either builds mutual trust, respect, and safety or tears it down for both participants. To understand that dynamic, it is useful to realize that dialogues or conversations have three levels of impact:

Three Levels of Conversational Impact

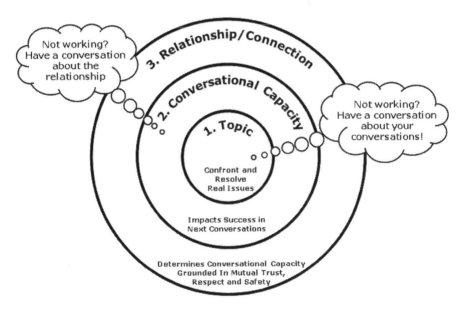

Level 1: *The Topic or Issue*   Impact: Effectiveness or Waste
When you intend progress, each conversation will involve either a productive interaction or a lack of results related to the topic or issue. When results have not been produced and forward movement is missing, your conversation has produced a waste of time and energy.

Level 2: *Conversational Capacities*   Impact: Increased or Decreased
Each interaction you have with another person impacts your capacity to have further conversations that work. The skills required—which we call **Conversational Capacities**—build over time and improve with practice just like the muscle memory athletes build when practicing skills related to their particular sport. It is easier to continue in patterns where you have past-based, unproductive muscle memory and strength because they are usually unconscious and have been heavily practiced. If you don't practice new skills and build new, productive muscle memory for your interactions, you slip into habits that haven't worked in the past and aren't going to work in the next conversation either.

Level 3: *The Relationship*   Impact: Built Up or Torn Down
The quality of a relationship tends to be the sum total of your experience in interactions and conversations. For others, each conversation with you contributes to their mental File Cabinet about you, categorizing the level of productivity possible in working with you and the overall quality of the relationship you share. Your interactions either deepen the relationship or take it down several notches.

With so much at stake, no wonder so many people consider that it is better to just avoid the conversation completely—or at least avoid certain topics or individuals where our experience tells us it might not go well! Fear of making the situation worse, uncertainty about how to handle resistance, or concern about negatively impacting the relationship has many people avoid, capitulate, or become superficial and gratuitous in their conversations. They leave the real issue safely undisturbed and sadly unresolved.

The problem with avoidance or trying hard not to make waves is that you will generally get what you are trying to avoid. The longer-term impact is the same (or worse) as if you took on the topic or conversation and failed! The real issue or topic does not even have a chance to get forwarded, let alone resolved. At the level of conversational capacities, no new conversational muscles are built and, worse, you are overtraining your avoidance muscle! Finally, relationships weaken and become superficial. Real safety goes out the window and collaboration breaks down in the delusion of what superficially appeared to be a safer path. The cycle continues as the next issue or topic pops up. No conversational capacities are built, relationships are diminished, and there is a loss of hope for effective resolution.

Three Emotional Zones

The next illustration shows three possible emotional zones you could be in when you are communicating with others: Comfort Zone, Learning Zone, and Distress-Upset Zone. Successfully upgrading your own collaborative capacities requires expanding your Learning Zone through stretching your own Comfort Zone to include previously distressing or upsetting conversations. It means stepping beyond your previously self-imposed limits—the places where you held back or stopped. This intervention into your previously predictable patterns will greatly impact your success in leading and thriving in the face of fear, resistance, and unrelenting change.

Three Emotional Zones

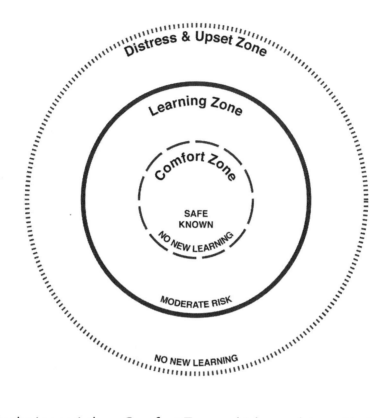

In the inner circle or **Comfort Zone**, which correlates with the center line in our Leadership Choice Point illustration, you feel safe and comfortable, take no risks, and no real learning, growth, or expansion of conversational capacities takes place. When you step out of your Comfort Zone into the **Learning Zone,** take a risk, learn something new, and expand your Conversational Capacities, real learning and skill building occurs. Your Comfort Zone then grows over time as you become competent with new interaction skills that used to be uncomfortable for you, at best, and upsetting for you in the extreme.

The outer or **Distress-Upset Zone** is where you feel very stressed, way past uncomfortable, and in your survival mode—just as you do when you follow the lower line in the Leadership Choice Point illustration. No new learning or growth takes place in this zone either. We continually counsel clients that when one or more people in the conversation are operating from this Distress-Upset Zone, no effective collaboration is possible.

The only effective strategy when you or the interaction you are having falls into the Distress-Upset Zone is to stop asserting your agenda and focus on reconnecting with the other person. Persisting while in the Distress-Upset Zone will only drive the conversation deeper into a survival-based interaction. The topic or issue will get stuck, blown out of proportion, or completely derailed, and unproductive emotions will become the driving force. Conversational Capacities between the parties will rapidly diminish both during the incident and in subsequent interactions, and the relationship itself will be negatively impacted. Practice getting used to being uncomfortable, recognize it as a *Learning Zone Feeling*, identify what throws you into the Distress-Upset Zone, and rein yourself back to a curious, learning perspective. Have *another* conversation about that previously distressing topic and you will have expanded your Learning Zone and decreased the library of off-limits topics.

Daily conversations that stretch your previous capacities help build your conversational muscle. When you engage in a conversation covering tough issues and courageously confront and work through them with another person, you are creating the muscle memory and tone to be able to really flex and strengthen those capacities. You can be confident in your ability to address issues, solve problems, and creatively pursue opportunities together. As you gain experience with these types of successes, you will also find yourself having a new view of the relationship.

As shown in the circle illustration, if you don't push out of your Comfort Zone, you're stuck in stasis and no muscles get built. If you operate from the Distress-Upset Zone, you end up in unproductive stress and upset. The art of improving your conversational capacities lies in knowing how and when to push into the Learning Zone and increase it, eventually lessening the Distress-Upset Zone or moving it up and out into completely new territory.

Productive Dialogue

The purpose of dialogue is to create something new—something that has not been thought previously by any participant prior to the conversation.

Ultimately, our Yonder Star in writing this book is to enable you and others to engage in **Productive Dialogues** (as opposed to simple cooperation) as a route to effective collaboration in the face of fear, resistance, and unrelenting change. This term applies to interactions that take place in an environment where participants feel safe enough to really address their own and others' issues and are taking responsibility for making the dialogue a success. This applies equally to your interactions at work, within your other groups and associations, and certainly in your family!

Successful collaboration (whether in business or personal life) is built with Productive Dialogue and has several essential elements. It is important that participants are:

- aligned and focused on a shared Yonder Star;

- connected to one another and interacting as team members—on the same team, rather than as adversaries;

- creating an atmosphere of mutual trust, respect, and safety;

- openly sharing knowledge, information, and resources;

- getting present to the current condition;

- generating forward movement with clarity and accountability.

The model that represents how Productive Dialogues work is shown below. While there is nothing inherently wrong with conversing in either circle, some of the potential approaches are far less valuable than others. In the **Productive Dialogue Zone**, interactions become very productive and real ground is taken in fulfilling your Yonder Star.

Productive Dialogue Zone

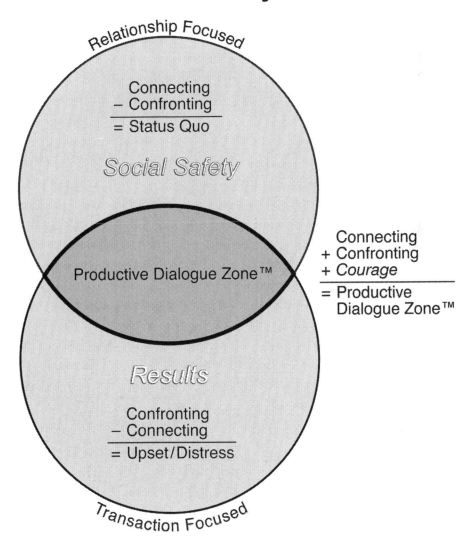

Definitions:

> **Connecting:** *To be related, in the present moment; to meet the other person's world (literally, to bind or bond with; from con, "with," and nexus, "bind").*
>
> **Confronting:** *To stand in front of something (the real issue) together, to address a "gap" with another person or group. To move the conversation "up and out" toward the Yonder Star.*
>
> **Courage:** *To step into a conversation with intention and without knowing how to get back out of it, let alone how to fulfill your Yonder Star for the relationship! Courage is a prerequisite. (Courage is the presence and effect, -age, of heart, cour).*

Transaction Based Conversations—Results over Relationship

The lower circle depicts interactions that are transaction based—their purpose is intensely focused on achieving a specific goal, often to the exclusion of concern for connection or relatedness. Participants aren't really connecting with each other, force is the order of the day, and results are all that really matter. "Getting in their faces" is deemed OK, because, after all, it's about getting the job done! An undesirable outcome of interacting in this mode in the extreme is generating fear and a survival-brain response from others, depicted by the lower line of the Leadership Choice Point and the outer Distress-Upset Zone circle in the Emotional Zones graphic. Results are not particularly creative or innovative, and the likelihood of collaboration and accountability is greatly diminished. Instead, these disconnected interactions can generate malicious compliance. This happens most often when you are pushing your agenda, perhaps passionately, without regard for the impact on the other person—not even noticing whether you are connected or they are hearing much of what you are saying. While important and useful in getting people out of a burning building, this leadership style seldom produces sustainably high creativity or ownership in fulfilling a team's Yonder Star.

Social Safety Conversations—Relationship over Results

The upper circle represents interactions in which there is a high level of socially focused interaction, connection and, in the extreme, being either inspirational or politically correct supersedes the importance of results. Participants attend first to the niceties of relating, carefully tiptoeing around thorny issues. Because they don't confront and deal with real issues, meaningful results are slow to happen or not produced at all, thereby maintaining the status quo. Fear is at work in this circle also—fears of losing regard or respect or the relationship itself. This behavior pattern reflects complicity between the parties to stay in the Comfort Zone, not rocking the boat with a thorny issue or difficult conversation! At some point, the lack of forward movement often pushes people to a high level of frustration followed by a jump to the lower circle when the missing results become intolerable.

Productive Dialogue Zone—Results *and* Relationship

> *Be someone who facilitates the growth of collaborative capital*

In the Productive Dialogue Zone where the two circles overlap, people pay attention to both being connected *and* producing outcomes. Participants bring themselves to the interaction with a mind-set of value creation for themselves and others, making the situation safe *and* productive and being responsible for what gets heard. They make meaningful strides in fulfilling the Yonder Star. Practitioners who have learned to skillfully apply this model are mindful of the importance of being connected and in relationship before any real, especially threatening, issues can be addressed. They focus on confronting issues rather than confronting other participants in the discussion and on being sure real outcomes are produced from the interaction. In this type of conversation, participants walk away with solutions and high regard for themselves and each other.

Many leaders strive to build a winning team by collecting a group of smart individuals with great resumes and experience. What they have, to start, is great *intellectual capital*—the sum of all of the resumes. However, the sum of the parts does not guarantee a powerfully effective team. There are many examples of sports teams that, despite an amazing collection of skillful athletes, don't win championships and, conversely, sports teams with a collection of mostly "unknowns" who win championships through their impressive teamwork.

When *individuals* have developed themselves to work effectively in the Productive Dialogue Zone, we say that they have a high level of **collaborative capacities**. This essential leadership skill distinguishes those who are known as individual high performers from those who have developed many top performers around themselves. When *groups* have developed themselves to work effectively in the Productive Dialogue Zone, we say they have created a high level of **collaborative capital** that is as real as other assets on an organization's balance sheet. A team that regularly and reliably generates creative, innovative and effective solutions has greater collaborative capital than the sum of the capacities of all of the individuals involved.

Operating Principles— A Systemic Shift

Principle: A basic premise guiding personal conduct

Operating Principles: A system of premises guiding thinking, listening, speaking, and actions

What Is the Nature and Purpose of Operating Principles?

Applying the Operating Principles will actually redesign and guide your thinking, listening, speaking, and actions in new ways appropriate to fulfilling your Yonder Star. By choosing this approach, you actually reframe or upgrade the design of the operating system in your mind that has been in place for many years. These principles underlie and give life to a new context for your conversations. We will address when it is appropriate to apply the Operating Principles and when it isn't later in the book.

You *can* design a conversation intentionally, although most people don't. Most conversations have a design that is invisible and unconscious. The Operating Principles cause powerful and productive interventions into conventional thinking, ways of being, and interaction. Our Operating Principles are designed to create a context that shapes *you* in the process. They work as a system to support a safe, creative, productive workspace in which to raise and resolve issues. Employing them successfully requires a shift from status quo, all-knowing confidence, rigidity, and judgment to what David Whyte calls "an investigative vulnerability." This conscious shift includes the qualities of curiosity, connection, presence, and open-minded learning—as well as courage, choice, and practice. They have evolved over years of observation, input from others, and practice—by us, as well, as thousand of clients and students.

The result is a group of principles that move you from constantly being the victim of unexamined beliefs, emotional reactions, and the circumstances of your situation to a person who can claim your power.

One of our participants likes to say, "I'm at choice!" When you inform your choices, actions, and conversations with the Operating Principles and your Yonder Star, you experience a new world of Self-Generated Accountability and collaborative interactions. In this way, you become a safe ally, an attractive force, and a person around whom others can raise issues and resolve them productively.

Why Did We Choose Operating Principles versus Rules?

We actually started out focusing on a simple set of rules for groups and workshops, some of which were as basic as "be on time" and "no side talk." When we used these, not much interesting developed at any higher level in the group discussions. Over the years and as a result of Suzanne's speaking experience, we have observed other groups who use different types of guidelines and get a variety of outcomes. For example, we have noted that some groups who have "clubhouse rules" tend to have a clubhouse type of culture.

Why Did We Choose Operating Principles versus Agreements?

We upgraded from Operating Rules to Operating Agreements fairly quickly and noticed some improvement in effect. Although the element of agreement brought some new energy, the parental nature of rules surged right back with the idea of "you have agreed." While that was not all bad, we were looking for more. The new flaw was that the word *agreement* actually invoked an "agree-disagree" mentality and seemed to focus attention on participants' judgments and opinions, based on the contents of their own individual File Cabinets. We were actually seeking a much deeper intervention that would give participants new access to more powerful thought processes and effective interactions. Such were the early seeds of Self-Generated Accountability.

It took a few more years of learning and evolution of the principles into forms more like those we have today. One day one of our long-term colleagues, Jim Bergquist of Business Futures Consulting, was reading through our latest version and said, "Hey, these things are not agreements and you'd better quit calling them that. They are fundamental principles that guide the design of conversations and are actually fairly deep interventions into people's conventional paradigm. It's time to step up the way you deliver them." We did and continue to be grateful to Jim for this suggestion.

As we worked more and more successfully with the more recent sets of Operating Principles, we began to see and speak of them as a system. During regular reviews and sharing about outcomes, clients and group members frequently pointed to how much all of the principles intertwine and how different dimensions open up for people as they engage with each of them. Sometimes we would reduce the number and users would protest. On the other hand, we constantly weeded out partial or whole principles that did not stand the test of time and experience. We observed that the surviving individual principles, grouped together, were working as a system and producing the desired effects.

Some of our clients ask, "Doesn't it take two? What good does it do for me to learn to interact more productively if the other person won't go there? Maybe after they have done your program or had your coaching, *then* I can try to have a productive conversation with them!" Our response is to offer the perspective of one of our colleagues, Nikky Nemerouf, who asks, "What are you more in control of in life...what you get from it or what you bring to it?"

We're not going to pretend that everyone is going to work with you, and we're certainly not going to say it's easy to engage newly with someone on a topic that has not gone well or has been stuck in the past. The two of you have history together. You each have expectations of how it's going to go. Not only do you each have all of your own unexamined patterns, you have also trained each other in previous interactions. If you are willing to commit to shifting the unproductive pattern or predictable failure, you can make huge progress in most situations.

If you are willing to step up to leadership in the interaction, you can cause breakthroughs by shifting your own mind-set and approach. This book is about giving you access to leadership practices for a new world. You'll have to step up and step in.

At this point let's focus on a couple of the key points. First, be willing to consider that the other person may well be responding to your past behavior and approach. Second, be willing to open up and be more vulnerable without waiting for the other person to do so or, worse, attempting to coerce them to open up without any new opening from you. Give up trying to fix them. You can save a lot of frustration, pain, and wasted energy if you give up trying to consciously fix other people without their permission. Fixing doesn't work and you will almost certainly anger them, chase them away, or both.

Work on using the Operating Principles to bring yourself to each situation and conversation more productively, and notice how the situation shifts. As you build confidence and competence with the Operating Principles, you retrain yourself. By modeling new effectiveness, your circle of friends and acquaintances will begin to trust that significant issues can be brought up and resolved with you. They will also experience that it is safe to be creative and open with you.

> In the emerging field of social neuroscience, researchers are using functional MRIs to discover how our brains interlock with others during our interactions with them and to study the resultant cascading impact on our biology, chemistry, and even immune system. They refer to the "social brain," the neural circuitry that operates as we interact. Previously, neuroscience studied only one brain at a time. Now two are analyzed at once, unveiling what Daniel Goleman, in his book *Social Intelligence*, calls a "neural duet between brains as people interact." This exciting new field of research brings scientific explanations and insight into the physiological and health impacts we have experienced ourselves and observed with our clients as the result of interactions with others.

These recent studies are consistent with our own experiential observations. They also provide further evidence supporting the value of giving up trying to change others and instead bringing yourself to your interactions in a new, more productive manner. Based on this data from social neuroscience, your new approach will actually have your intended positive impact on the brain circuitry and health of others!

Stop and consider the impact you are currently having (whether you realize it or not) on the health, well-being, and creative capacities of those around you. Ask yourself if you would be willing to hold yourself accountable for *causing* the behaviors you observe in others when they are around you. Listen carefully to your internal dialogue here. We are not saying you are to blame. We are saying that how you think, speak, listen, and act *influences* how others think, speak, listen, and act with respect to you. You are part of a neural duet. Taking on the Operating Principles to guide your interactions will set up an alternative way of being and interacting that can give you new insights into how and when your interactions succeed and fail.

How Do Operating Principles Intervene and Cause New Outcomes?

We have already introduced the metaphor of your brain as a File Cabinet with your own unique lifelong memories, experiences and emotions, judgments, and beliefs. The physical brain shares many characteristics with personal computers. Both are physical objects that run on electricity and compute. Effective use of the brain requires language in all forms, including pictures. The type of language we load in as children influences our lives as adults. Differing languages guide individuals to different thought and behavior patterns. From this perspective, an Asian, for example, may think quite differently about a situation than a European due to their linguistic structures. Human brains can be likened to computers that run on language, which includes words, pictures, records of emotions, and thought patterns that have been created and stored in our mental File Cabinets. Mental pictures, stored thoughts about how things should have been, and past experiences, especially unpleasant ones in early life, shape our interactive capacities decades later.

These Operating Principles can become powerful interventions into the way you have thought and interacted in the past, which has been based on those stored records. This intervention will, in turn, alter the interpretation, meaning, and current impact or influence of those early experiences and give you a new relationship with your current experiences and interactions. This will open up your thinking and allow you to rapidly expand your adult learning and interactive capacities. With new capacities, you can create an environment of mutual trust, respect, and safety for yourself and others and dramatically reduce friction and waste in your interactions. At those moments when you become closed, defensive, or cut off from others, you will be prompted to be open to new ideas and points of view and have a way of thinking that facilitates your ability to take on and work through tough issues effectively. Applying the Principles requires *choice, presence, and courage* in the moment so that you can access these valuable mental upgrades rather than continue to react from automatic and largely unexamined past records. When integrated and used often, they revise your mental processes, creating a new and more effective "normal."

For Deep Integration—Practice with Intention

We are offering the opportunity for a significant intervention and transformation. We are not talking about a simple word-processing "search and replace" function where you just change your words, mimic back the ideas, or put a new look on an old concept. Your real intent and thoughts directly cause your body language, your speaking, and actions—all those things that people pay attention and react to when involved in interactions with you.

Enabling the Operating Principles to guide your intentions as well as your actions and cause new openings and possibilities in your conversations and relationships will require the deep integration that comes from continued practice. To get the most value from your increased capacities, incorporate the Operating Principles into your everyday life, both at work and at home. Only if you practice, practice, and then practice some more will you begin to see the effects on your interactions. Start by committing yourself to this process—or else just put the book back on the shelf and walk off or give it away!

Here is a complete list of our nine Operating Principles. Subsequent chapters will provide deeper explanation, examples, and opportunities for practice.

The Operating Principles

1. **Be Present, Stay in the Game**

2. **Listen Newly, Be Intentionally Slow to Understand**

3. **Take Myself Lightly**

4. **Declare There Is Nothing Wrong or Broken** *Here and Now*

5. **Explore** *truths*: **Mine, Theirs, and Ours**

6. **Confront and Deal with Real Issues**

7. **Be Responsible for Creating Value**

8. **Make It Safe** *and* **Productive**

9. **Be Responsible for What Gets Heard**

Section Two:

It Begins with Me

Self-Generated Accountability

If not me, then who? If not now, then when?

Adapted from old Hebrew adage

In an environment of unrelenting change, some of your greatest assets are your own awareness, creativity, and intention. Access to creativity and accomplishment will come from holding yourself responsible for your thoughts, speaking, listening, and actions and their associated influences and outcomes. Our essential notion of Self-Generated Accountability has, at its core, this personally aware and responsible nature of leadership and collaboration.

Self-Generated Accountability—*It Begins with Me!*

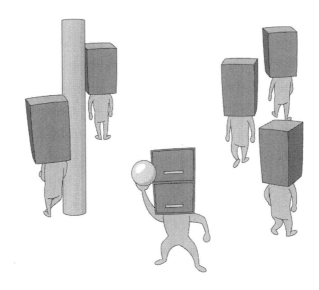

Accountability Examined

Most of our clients and program participants want more accountability around them and constantly search for the absence of it in others when things begin to go wrong. Sometimes this label of "more accountability" becomes a catchall phrase disguising the real issues.

When clients come up with more accountability as the solution, we find that they are often seeking reliability—or "people doing what they said they would do, by the time they said they would do it or, if not, at least letting me know that there is an issue in enough time to take another route."

The use of the term "accountability" can also come from a mental framework expressed as "*I* am going to hold *you* accountable" or "Managers *should* hold their people more accountable." If this common thought process and expression is actually applied, the real meaning is "Joe, if this project doesn't get done, it's your head, not mine." There is no collaboration, joint ownership, or sense of partnership for either party. The joke, of course, is that if your employee Joe fails or quits, you've *still* got the project, and the failure is still on your watch! Partner with Joe in confronting and resolving real issues instead of confronting Joe, the person. Joe will still be the one doing the work, only now he will have the benefit of your partnership and creativity in addressing the situation.

These unexamined ways of thinking about accountability set up conversations that are ineffective and disheartening, and make you and others sound like victims. If you really examine these ways of thinking and speaking, you will find that it lacks personal responsibility and any real, truly effective power.

> It is a common organizational myth that you or I can really hold someone else accountable for the kind of creativity, collaboration, and action that fulfills

Yonder Stars. At best you can dominate and control another person to where you get what one of our clients calls "vicious obedience." Obedience does not stimulate creative thinking, problem solving, or responsibility.

It Begins with Me!

Self-Generated Accountability dictates that you ask yourself these questions:

- What is it about the way I interact with others that gets in the way of these seemingly simple and straightforward requests being met?

- What stops people around me from operating that way with me all the time?

- What is missing?

- Am I really a victim of this apparent condition?

- Am I trapped "under the circumstances"?

Under the Circumstances!

We can hear your mind saying, "Yeah, but how *do* I get Joe to be more accountable?" This question does come up frequently; so later in the book we have included a practical application to use with another person to generate more accountability. Refer to Practical Application: *"Productive Delegation—Building Confidence and Accountability."*

First, we're concerned with upgrading *your* thought processes and consequent behaviors so that you are able to significantly increase both the direct influence and the ripple effect of your leadership. Give up trying to change others, at least for a short time, while you develop yourself through applying the material in this book and the practice opportunities. Concentrate on what you control, what you bring to life versus what you get from it.

Catch yourself shoving off responsibility to others simply by suggesting that others *should* be more accountable. Turn your finger-pointing right around, point at your own nose and ask yourself this question: "What is *my* contribution to this situation?" If your immediate, defensive answer is "nothing" or "but…but…they…" think again! It is significantly more challenging to your ego and self-righteousness to lead and influence from Vision-Focused Leadership than from a command and control paradigm.

> One of our colleagues related a story from the time she was accumulating her babysitting experience early in life. She was spending time with a precocious two-year-old who was consistently asserting her will regarding what she wanted to do or did not want to do—as many of us have experienced with toddlers of that age. While some of us may have heard, "You're not the boss of me" from children of that age, this child had a different take on the attitude. Her statement was "*I* am the boss of me!" That pretty much sums up the notion of Self-Generated Accountability, from the mouth of a babe!

No one else can ever truly hold you accountable, except to minimum standards of conformity. To put it in simple terms, you really are the Boss of You! To unleash your creativity, self-expression and passion for the work (and give the project the highest odds of being extraordinarily successful) the accountability has to be created in your shoes, over where you are, owned by you, and re-created when the going gets tough. If you do that, rather than looking for excuses for failure in the face of daunting circumstances, you will be looking for new strategies for delivering the project on time.

In this transformational shift to Self-Generated Accountability:

- you recognize the source of accountability, learn how to practice it for yourself, and how to help evoke it in others in the environment *you* create and support;

- you increase your ability to translate intentions into reality, starting from the point of view that you have a *choice* as to which of your thoughts turn into conversations and guide your actions;

- you recover your power—reclaiming it from others or from the circumstances, moving from impotent victim to responsible collaborator;

- you have the opportunity to choose, commit to, and communicate to others that part of a shared Yonder Star that *you* can be counted on to deliver.

Study the following three Operating Principles for valuable insights on how to incorporate Self-Generated Accountability into every moment and aspect of your life. Then practice, practice, practice.

Operating Principle #1:

Be Present, Stay in the Game

In this period in our cultural history, an increasing number of people are working to learn to be more present and engaged with all that is occurring around them at any given moment. In a shifting and changing world, having a solid grasp on the reality of the present moment puts you miles ahead of those floundering in delusion and doubt. High-performing athletes provide some of the best examples of this idea of being present. They have an amazing ability to focus only on the ball that is coming at them and know just what to do with it to score. They are not focused on the past or future or letting random thoughts invade their concentration. In fact, at moments of peak performance, there is no thinking going on, just action, as the players align all their actions with the Yonder Star of being a team, executing their moves to their very best ability, and getting the win. Top athletes often speak of this experience as being "in the zone."

The first step toward the goal of presence lies in recognizing that the past is gone, the future is not here yet, and the only place you really have a choice or can take action is in the present moment. This is a fundamental idea underlying this Operating Principle as well as our Leadership Choice Point model. An essential idea here is that you always have an opportunity to choose in the present and, in fact, it is the only time you actually have a choice! That defines the **choice point**—it's always available, right here, right now. If you are conscious and present in the moment, your awareness of your surroundings, your focus, and your conscious thoughts will play a major role in shaping your speaking and listening in that moment. Whatever is occupying your attention is reflected in your listening, speaking, and actions and actually designs your life experiences. If you are not present, your thoughts and actions may be much more shaped by the instant, automatic, and unexamined contents retrieved from your File Cabinet.

Leadership Choice Point

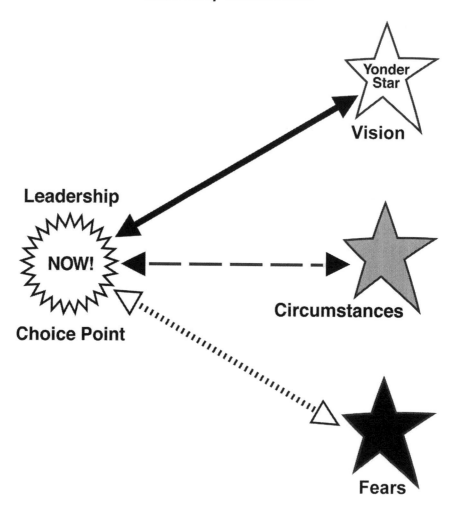

If you are solely focused on the past, the obstacles you have encountered that got in your way or stopped you may drive your current thoughts and actions. That focus can prevent you from opening up to being present in current reality and to new ideas as you move forward. A major limitation in times of unrelenting change is a propensity to repeat past experiences over and over in an environment that requires new solutions. That behavior is often said to be the definition of insanity. There is a parable in the book *Who Moved My Cheese* by Spencer Johnson, MD, of a mouse who keeps traveling down the "no cheese" path because that is where the cheese *used* to be.

The best thing about the future is that it comes only one day at a time.

Abraham Lincoln–*16ᵗʰ President of the United States*

If you are solely focused on the future, you are concerned about things that have not yet happened and may be missing what is going on right in front of your nose. President Lincoln was getting closer to the truth about the future. Eckhart Tolle points out in *A New Earth*, however, that the future never comes. It is only ever now—tomorrow it will be now! The idea of "future" is a concept that can keep you from being present in the moment. Whether you are dreaming of things being much better or are obsessing about something bad happening, you will not be armed with the power available from being present to the way things are and the way they are not.

> Our definition of worry: Create a distressing mental picture of a scenario that hasn't happened yet, and obsess on it right now!

If you are focused on that distressing mental picture, you are concerned about things that have not yet happened and may be missing what is going on right in front of your nose. Worse, you may miss many signals of good things that could happen, and you certainly won't be taking responsibility for inventing outcomes you love and taking action on them.

Choose your Focus—Your Yonder Star!

The big opportunity here is to envision a Yonder Star that fully expresses who you are and what you are committed to, whether it is for you as an individual or as a team. You may start by envisioning your intended outcomes or ideal situation at some future date. Envisioning it that way creates a new context to inform your thoughts, illuminates the gap between current circumstances and the desired state, and gives rise to new choices and actions. To influence your actions in the present, your Yonder Star does not continue to live as a future scenario. Since you can only act in the present, the ability to re-create or envision it in each moment is essential. Your Yonder Star continues informing your thoughts and actions and intervenes in what would otherwise be past-based thinking. That only occurs in the present. When it is fulfilled, it will be in the present. Being present to both your immediate circumstances and your Yonder Star allows you to shape your speaking and listening in new ways. Without a creative Yonder Star, the most likely outcome will be repetition of the past.

Your worries and concerns, haunting you from your mental File Cabinet past or your distressing "what if" future scenario, will not fully go away. They will slip to the periphery of your awareness and lose their grip on your thinking and attention when you displace that mind share with a focus on your Yonder Star *and* being present to the way that it is and isn't. When you do, you are choosing to correlate your actions with something you are consciously envisioning or creating, rather than being limited by circumstances or being driven by fear or unconscious emotional reactions.

What Takes You Away from Presence?

Let's face it; your brain runs much faster than you can talk. It is bound to be considering all sorts of things all the time, even while other people are speaking! Often, what takes you away from being fully present is getting lost in your File Cabinet. There is lots of information available to peruse, and your File Cabinet research, including your emotional reactions to what other people are saying, can occupy a great deal of your focus. We call these derailing internal focuses "mental and emotional barriers."

> Dwight met a Grand Prix driver once who had severe Attention Deficit Disorder. During his normal day, he could go to the garage for a screwdriver and be found there two hours later sweeping the floor or tinkering with the lawn mower. His brain jumped quickly from thing to thing and he followed. What he said, however, was "You'd be surprised how clear and quiet it gets when I'm running at 160 mph two feet off the wall." The pace of the action and a life-preserving demand for his attention was closer to keeping up with his mental activity.

Like the Grand Prix driver, you could be distracted on another matter that has grabbed your attention. Frequently, you are busy comparing and contrasting what the speaker is saying to your own File Cabinet records, thinking about whether you agree, disagree, or see potential roadblocks. The ability to be present is an essential capacity for working together effectively in the face of fear, resistance, and unrelenting change. It's a key component of your mental agility and effective performance capacities.

A recent example is the miraculous landing of US Airways Flight #1549 on the Hudson River in January 2009. For the pilot, Chesley B. "Sully" Sullenberger, being "cool, calm, and collected" each moment in the face of almost certain disaster, and with few options at his disposal, allowed him to be incredibly focused, lead his cockpit team, and execute the critical actions required to perform an essentially perfect water landing.

> From the *60 Minutes* "Miracle on the Hudson" segment with Katie Couric:
> Sullenberger: "The physiological reaction I had for this was strong and I had to force myself to use my training and force calm on the situation."

Katie Couric: "Was that a hard thing to do?"
Sullenberger: "No, it just took some concentration."

Checking your File Cabinet is instant, automatic, and unavoidable. You rely on this data and the speed of retrieval to be able to negotiate almost everything in life every day. You would not know how to get home at night if you could not check your File Cabinet to make sure you have arrived at the right house. You need this stored information to have intelligent interactions with your co-workers, family, and friends. It becomes problematic when you get stuck in your own File Cabinet, insisting that it contains the only true or right way to do things. Using your stored data to fend off or dismiss new ideas will disconnect you from those around you, diminish your ability to lead, and rob you of any real ability to stimulate creative conversations.

Closed-minded!
No New Learning

Get Back in the Game!

We will all fail at this operating principle quite regularly. No need for pretense, just get back in the game. When you are working in a group and notice that your thoughts are drifting away, acknowledge it. Sit forward, raise your hand, and say, "I'm sorry, I drifted out and I really want to hear what you just said, so could you repeat it?" This not only brings you back and honors the speaker's contribution to the group, it reminds others to check their own thoughts and pay more attention to being present. It makes it safer for them to acknowledge their own drifting.

> *Tip: Create a Mini Yonder Star*
>
> If you invent a mini Yonder Star, a mental picture of getting extraordinary value for yourself from the meeting or speaker at hand, the pull of envisioning *that* star will provide focus for your attention. Your mind goes to work quite faithfully fulfilling these pictures you described to yourself. You will be listening for value without ever consciously thinking about it.

Using "I" Statements

Using "I" statements focuses me on my own words and experience rather than a generalized statement, opinion, or story about society at large.

The use of "I" statements is essential to having productive interactions and setting up an environment of mutual trust, respect, and safety. It signals ownership and helps prevent defense. This recommendation supports a number of the Operating Principles. We are introducing it here in the context of this operating principle as a means to help create presence for yourself and others.

We sometimes get push back for this recommendation for using "I" statements by people repeating the cliché "There is no 'I' in 'team.'" We are not talking about an ego-driven strategy to self-aggrandize. To be fair, we recognize that there is an egocentric and extremely unproductive use of "I" by some people to claim credit, grab territory, or promote themselves in another's eyes. A classic example is the manager who reads a report by one of his direct reports and then introduces the best ideas as his own when in a meeting. We are talking about a very different and important use other than grabbing credit.

Speaking in the first person regarding observations, beliefs, and points of view expresses your ownership of your statement and makes it real for the listener. It also makes you more accountable for what you say. If you doubt that, watch how often even experienced practitioners will switch from "I" statements to "you" statements, or even refer to themselves in the second person, when what they are saying feels risky or emotional for them. When you preface your statement with "you" instead of "I," it presents an opinion or story rather than a shared experience, inviting your listeners to tune out. Statements that could be powerful as a shared experience, and yet are said as "you" or the regal "we," are a way of reducing risk, being detached from the statement, and subconsciously feeling you can more easily make your escape if the conversation goes badly. Using "you" statements can also distract other brains, sending them into their File Cabinets to assess whether the statement you just made is actually true for them. In the worst-case scenario, "you" statements can occur as an attack, activating primitive **survival brain** responses and blocking access to productivity.

Why is Being Present Important?

> *The ability to be in the present moment is a major component of mental wellness.*

Abraham Maslow–*American Psychologist noted for his conceptualization of a "hierarchy of human needs"*

When you are present, you can acknowledge your File Cabinet data *and at the same time* be receptive to adding to or revising it. In that space where participants are present and open, the dialogue can be resourceful and creative, generating new solutions that previously did not exist in either File Cabinet prior to the dialogue. An ability to be present in the midst of chaos or uncertainty separates great leaders from those who get caught up in the swirl of group panic or fear-based knee-jerk reactions. It makes a difference between muddled thinking and clear, thoughtful, decisive action.

That's not to say that being present is always easy or comfortable. In fact, we notice our clients frequently engage in distractions of various types to avoid the:

- high levels of uncertainty they face;

- frequency and volume of emotional issues to be dealt with on a daily basis;

- increasing demands for immediate action;

- sheer volume of communications coming at them.

It could even be said that the sometimes desperate drive for control is an attempt to avoid the pain and confusion generated by the "sacred messiness of life." The practice that seems to be escalating the quickest is the demand for instant communication. Leaders who demand this behavior from team members, tolerate it from clients, or simply fall into it themselves risk being more and more disconnected from the present, from thinking and relationships, and from the creative processes required to be strategic.

A few of the unexamined diversion tactics to avoid being present:

- being in constant reaction mode to cell phones and BlackBerries ringing and vibrating and the corollary expectation that employees be in constant and instant communication;

- treating every phone call, e-mail, text message, or even heads bobbing into the doorway as more important than the matter at hand—often describing it as effective multitasking;

- demanding obsessive amounts of detail, asking for yet another analysis;

- insisting on exclusively rational notions, or in some cases cutting off all discussion.

What Difference Does It Make?

When you are listening, being present focused, and really aware of what someone is saying and how the person is choosing to express thoughts, you get the full content of the message much more quickly. In addition, a deeper level of information will be available to you. Being present while listening is essential to generating a **productive environment** of mutual trust, respect, and safety. It lessens the space between you and the other person, and makes you available to truly connect and create a rapport with another. The most powerful dialogues occur when you listen and remain completely present and open to what a speaker is saying. It takes less time, not more, to get to the real issue and solutions. It helps eliminate waste in dialogues. In the experience of others, your intentional presence occurs as respect and often appreciation. Your own opportunity to be heard and appreciated is actually enhanced by your willingness and ability to be present with others. Try this one at home!

When speaking, being present means you choose to respond rather than react, letting go of emotions and objections and remaining focused on what is to be achieved. One of the simplest and yet most powerful ways to keep yourself present and in the game is to phrase your contributions to the discussion as "I" statements. This will demonstrate that you own your perspective and views and are not looking to push responsibility off onto anyone else. It will also contribute to keeping an intense conversation from derailing into defense.

When Being Present Is Missing:

- You welcome any distraction that pulls you away, or you look for an escape route—checking your BlackBerry becomes an urgent necessity.

- When you hear someone talking, you do an instant "Google" search of your File Cabinet to see if you agree or can help with a solution from your past— disconnecting you from truly listening. We call this "solution listening". Unfortunately, your own File Cabinet "Google" search often pulls up some very poor matches and sends your listening and speaking down irrelevant bunny trails.

- You get emotionally triggered and dwell in that mode.

- You avoid owning your own statements by speaking in second-person "you" statements or implying the agreement of others with "we" statements.

When This Principle Is in Play:

- You bring your concentration fully to what is happening around you, pulling yourself back from distracting thoughts and remaining open to all input. If you notice that you are automatically in your File Cabinet, you pause, thank your mind for the research, and get back to the present.

- If you think of something else that could be important, you quickly jot it down or make a mental note so then you can refocus on what is being said.

- You listen patiently, attuned to the total content *and* meaning. You don't try to formulate solutions, responses, or opinions yet.

- You use "I" statements, owning what you say and supporting the focus of the other minds in the room.

Case Study: Be Present, Stay in the Game

Learning to Connect

Joe had an ambition of becoming the chief operating officer and eventually chief executive officer of his company. The CEO wanted Joe to significantly grow in his leadership to really be a viable succession candidate. Joe gave thoughtful, well-prepared presentations; however, when the executive team began discussing issues that he felt did not apply to him, he often appeared "lost in his thoughts," inattentive, and disconnected. He was one of the people who would often tune out and use his Blackberry in his lap. He considered that behavior to be "productively multi-tasking" and couldn't understand why he didn't have a more collaborative working relationship with his peers.

Joe often complained that his direct reports were ineffective and uncommunicative. Feedback from his direct reports indicated that he was great at giving clear, concise directions up front and yet there was little chance for them to check in with him regarding issues along the way. They did not consider him to be approachable or feel that their input made any difference. When they attempted meetings with Joe he often continued answering emails, assuring them he could listen at the same time.

Bringing these blind spots to Joe's attention was not initially well received. He wanted to explain (defend) his behavior and point outside himself for the cause in his peers and direct reports. Because Joe was very committed to growing his leadership capacities, he eventually listened to what he could change about his approach and practices. Learning to be present, with full attention was very painful for Joe in the beginning. He had to give up his long held belief that it is more valuable (for him) to multi-task and realize that being present and really connecting is the key to interacting productively with others and producing greater outcomes for the whole team.

Case Study: Be Present, Stay in the Game

Suzanne—Shocked to Attention

When my daughter was eleven years old, we had a long drive home from school. After a hectic day at work, it was common for me to be a bit preoccupied thinking about my day, solving and resolving issues that had arisen, and thinking through my "to do" list for the next day.

On one of those days, I heard my daughter exclaim, "Suzanne!" (Guess I hadn't been hearing "Mom.") That brought me instantly present, paying attention, and looking over at her. She followed with, "You haven't been listening to me!" I instantly, automatically, and defensively reacted with, "Sure I have, honey!" She answered, "No, you haven't, Mom, because I just told you that I was pregnant and on drugs!" That froze me for a moment before I could ask, "You're not really, are you?" Thankfully, she answered, "No, Mom, I was just seeing if I could get your attention by being really dramatic!" She is now twenty-six, has never used drugs and has not yet been pregnant, so we can both look back on that conversation now and laugh about it.

The interaction we had that day was a defining moment for me; a wake-up call in a situation that was, fortunately, not serious, desperate, or out of control. I really saw how it might play out later in our relationship if she did have a really serious topic she wanted to talk about with me. I examined the capacities of our conversations that were being built (or not) and the limited level of my overall availability in the relationship. I got reconnected and became present to my Yonder Star for our relationship. From that point forward, I considered our drives home to be a special, private, precious time. I stayed present to the opportunity to be connected about our lives, our concerns, and our celebrations. Being present and staying in the game with her and with everyone else in my life became a discipline I have practiced ever since.

Practice Opportunities:
Be Present, Stay in the Game

Practice Being Present in Your Daily Life

Think of this principle the next time you find yourself:

- in a meeting;
- in an interaction with a colleague;
- in a conversation with a family or community member.

In each situation do the following:

1. In the midst of a distraction or examination of your own point of view, catch yourself.
2. Shift back to the present moment, in a curiosity mode, and connect with the others.
3. Get back in the game—if appropriate, acknowledge the distraction out loud and ask for restatement.

Notice what happens as a result—for you, for others, and the quality of the conversation. Note: These are situations where your mind may run much faster than the other person speaks. Recall the earlier tip for staying present and focused. Create a quick Yonder Star for the conversation or meeting, and let it keep you focused. It's also generally OK to ask for clarification to pull both of you back into focus if you are drifting.

Operating Principle #2:

Listen Newly, Be Intentionally Slow to Understand

Being fully listened to often translates to feeling respected.

The first Operating Principle, *Be Present, Stay in the Game*, is a pre-requisite to practicing this next Operating Principle. It is not possible to listen newly without being present. As you concentrate on your listening, allow your conscious focus on being present and listening for value to displace distracting thoughts that pull you away from the conversation.

Authentic Curiosity

When you were a young child, if you heard something new from a teacher, parent, or friend, you most likely listened intently, absorbing what was said, and asked lots of questions. These are good examples of what we call **Exploration Listening**, where you are authentically curious, connected to the other person, open, and focused on what he or she has to say. Rather than just absorbing the information imparted, you are alert to all the verbal and nonverbal cues that allow you to get beyond the content to understand the feelings, emotions, and intention or purpose behind the words.

◇◇◇

I have been really encouraged by practicing this and listening without a planned response. That trap of planning my response means I miss so much of the conversation. By staying present in the conversation, I often surprise myself with additional insight.

Tom Mullin–*Vice President of Engineering and New Product Development MicroAire Surgical Instruments LLC*

◇◇◇

This principle simply says: Choose an attitude of wonderment, taking in all that is being said without assuming you already know what the speaker is talking about. Let go of jumping ahead to finish his or her thoughts. Notice as your mind offers ideas and opinions from your File Cabinet and then set them aside for just a moment. Be patient and listen. Since brains work quickly with a lot of precognitive thought, being intentionally slow to understand doesn't have to take a long time—just a nanosecond longer than an instant, automatic reaction. That momentary suspension of the natural jump to conclusions allows you to keep your mind open to new ideas and concepts, so you are truly "listening newly." One of our Vistage Chair colleagues describes this as "listening with every pore." Be willing to suspend any tendency to a know-it-all persona, invoke an "investigative vulnerability," and ask questions which invite others to further develop their ideas or perspectives.

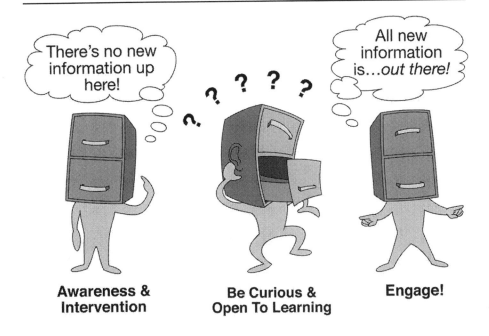

Awareness & Intervention

Be Curious & Open To Learning

Engage!

Ignore, Dispute, or Engage and Build

In order to learn you have to risk change...changing your mind!

Choose your listening! A common practice we observe that doesn't work very well is ignoring what another person just said and starting in on your own monologue that may or may not connect to what they just said. Another is disagreeing with what another person said, thereby taking the conversation to a positional focus on who and what is right—whose File Cabinet has the *right* stuff in it. In "disagree mode" you lose sight of the real issue and the issue at hand becomes convincing and converting the other person to your viewpoint. As a conscious alternative you can take a risk, listen newly, and engage with what is being said. It is risky to listen newly. Once you really let in what another person is saying, your File Cabinet is changed forever. The other person has now influenced even what you may say next. The opportunity, of course, is that the conversation becomes collaborative and creative.

A Self-Management Practice

When engaged in a discussion where someone is expressing his or her viewpoint, notice any "I agree" or "I disagree" thoughts you are having. If these pop up, it's a sure sign that you are not listening fully. You are already in your File Cabinet searching for a match to something you believe so you can deny or affirm the speaker's comment. You have disconnected and have limited your reception to any new thoughts or ideas. Thank your brain for its research and refocus outside your own thoughts to the person who is speaking and your Yonder Star for the meeting or interaction. Learn to trust that new ideas and new ways of working together to fulfill a shared Yonder Star may emerge from conversations where the agree/disagree dynamic has been suspended.

Only when you are more committed to the success of the project or relationship ("up and out") than to your own ego, getting credit, or being right, will you be able to successfully implement this Operating Principle.

Five Types of Unproductive, Disconnected Listening

Early in the development of our Productive Interactions Program, Suzanne decided to do additional experimentation around what she had been learning about our internal voice and its impact on our thoughts and reactions. (If you are asking yourself, while reading this passage, "What internal voice?" that's it…that's your internal voice!) Unbeknownst to Dwight, Suzanne decided to use her conversations with him as one of her experiments! Here are the five forms of unproductive listening/internal voice monologues she discovered in the process:

1. Critical Listening—"Why did you do it that way?" "That doesn't make sense." "You shouldn't have done that in the first place!" While not a new discovery, I have often explained these kinds of comments away as "only wanting the best for you" or "If I don't point it out to you who will?"

2. Solution Listening—I am busy searching my File Cabinet brain for the answer to his dilemma while he is talking, and I am impatiently waiting for him to finish so I can give him my brilliant solution. It is not a bad thing to want to help him out, or to wait until he finishes instead of interrupting. The unproductive piece is that I have disconnected and am busy doing File Cabinet research and haven't even heard all he has said. Furthermore, he may not even be looking for "help" from me!

3. The 1-2 Combo Listening—Frequently I combine my critical little voice with my solution voice, and in an instant my thoughts move from "that's not the way you should have done it" to "I know how to fix it."

4. Me Too Listening—This listening/internal voice pattern also involves diving into my File Cabinet and disconnecting from the speaker. Have you ever had someone ask you about your vacation, and as you start answering they jump in with their own story? They are not connected with you, not hearing or experiencing your sharing.

5. Competitive/Arrogant Listening—In this form of listening filter, my internal voice is saying, "That's nothing, I drove in traffic three hours to get here," or "I've been to China many more times, so I think I know a thing or two about it."

In all of these forms of listening, her internal voice filters were either disconnecting or judging or both. What was really surprising was how many unconscious, disconnecting, or judging internal conversations were going on, even in relatively benign conversations with a person in a great relationship. An insight from the experiment in addition to the five categories of unproductive listening was a realization that the listening filters had less to do with Dwight or the topic or the situation and everything to do with her own deeply engrained habits of mind. What our internal voice and thought patterns come up with first largely dictates what comes out of our mouths next. Even if you are good enough to shift the words you use, somehow the critical, judging message still gets across. The opportunity is to catch and interrupt those automatic patterns so that you can generate the kind of caring, supportive, and productive conversations that lead to the quality of relationships you intend to have.

> How do you listen? What are your listening filters? What is your internal voice saying when others are speaking? Do you notice patterns with certain people or around certain topics? In order to listen newly you have to be able to be present and right there with the other person rather than in your File Cabinet. Listening powerfully is a critical human connection and collaboration skill as well as a key leadership practice.

Why Is Listening Newly Important?

This way of listening helps you practice the first Operating Principle, *Be Present, Stay in the Game.* You screen out distracting thoughts that pull you away from the conversation. As you concentrate your listening, your focus becomes other-centered, outside your File Cabinet. Your intentional, fully present state allows you to more completely understand others' File Cabinets and viewpoints. Your ability to collaborate most effectively is enhanced when you are able to hear what is said and also what is unsaid. Context is even more important than content. Gaining mental self-control to displace preconceived notions that color your listening will greatly enhance your effectiveness. You will be able to engage in brainstorming new ideas and be able to see the larger picture that results from a collage of thoughts, ideas, and perspectives.

The expression "jumping to conclusions" describes what our instant and automatic File Cabinet does and is the *opposite* of this Operating Principle.

What Difference Does It Make?

When you begin to listen newly, you'll begin to fully connect with people, hearing and understanding what they are saying. By listening openly and newly and being intentionally slow to understand, you are helping to create a productive environment where collaboration gets easier and easier. The ability to completely focus, displace preconceived notions, and really hear from others reduces friction and waste. As you listen to others and they in turn pick up the cues and start listening better, you pave the way for getting to the real heart of the issues you are addressing. Creativity begins to flow between you. Other people can get interested in your input *after* they feel they have been heard and fully understood. Fulfillment of your shared Yonder Star will increase in velocity and you will have a lot more fun.

When Listening Newly Is Missing:

- You "already know."

- There are multiple monologues—everyone is tightly holding on to his or her own File Cabinet, not willing to cede his or her viewpoint or recognize any others.

- You don't even notice that some participants are sitting quietly, resigned in a belief that it won't make a difference if they contribute.

- You cut off the speaker with, "Oh, I know what you mean," or "I agree/disagree with that," quickly shutting down open interchange of ideas and further exploration.

- You are not present—so add all of the symptoms here from the first Operating Principle!

When This Principle Is in Play:

- You displace instant judgment with curiosity.

- Your mind-set is respectful, curious, open, exploring, and learning.

- You hear each contribution, being fully present in the moment.

- You manage your over-active mind that compels you to push the buzzer for your turn to talk, giving your brain an assignment to listen for content and context.

- People who were reluctant to say anything start speaking up, appreciating your attention and curiosity.

- The dialogue digs deeper into the real heart of the matter and results are produced with less effort and struggle.

Case Study: Listen Newly, Be Intentionally Slow to Understand

Cold Case Reopened

What if the world doesn't work the way you think it does?

Pete was very rigid in his views and very controlling in his interactions. I had a difficult time working with him in our regular one-to-one executive coaching sessions each month. Naturally, Pete was just as frustrated with the sessions as I was, and the more I looked for openings to have learning conversations ("pry"), the more frustrated and rejecting Pete would become.

One morning after about an hour and a half, Pete began to somewhat angrily pack his stuff, complaining that the one-to-one sessions were just a waste of his time. As he began to get up and walk out, I asked, "Pete, what if the world doesn't work the way you think it does?" Amazingly, Pete froze and then sat back down in silence. After what seemed like forever, perhaps thirty seconds, he said, "Now *that's* an idea worth discussing. Let's explore that for our next several sessions!" He had finally opened up to listening to and engaging with new ideas that challenged the way he had been viewing life and business. He began to listen newly and also take time to reflect and consider new ideas rather than instantly agree or dismiss them. He has become able to hear much more varied input and to consider more possibilities for his own actions, making him a more effective decision maker and leader.

Case Study: Listen Newly, Be Intentionally Slow to Understand

Suzanne—Uncovering a Common Yonder Star

Dwight and I first met at work where I had a position at the corporate office and Dwight managed field operations. After the first couple of years of corporate office versus the field struggles, our collegial relationship was strained, to say the least. Rather than rapport or professional appreciation, we shared mutual antagonism. We had what I would label "irreconcilable professional differences." His field perspective gave him much more appreciation for what it took to make things happen remotely and how often the best laid plans from "corporate" rarely survived their collision with reality. My corporate office perspective gave me a front seat view of the consequences that actions in the field had on aggregate corporate results and investor confidence.

During recreation time at an executive retreat, Dwight and I were matched up as ski lift partners on several long chair lift rides. During that time we discovered that we were both committed to the same vision, or Yonder Star as we use the term today. We both took the opportunity to listen newly, deeper and longer than our own points of view had previously allowed, and to really consider each other's perspectives. We discovered that we shared the same goals, while differing greatly on pathways for pursuit, measures of success along the way, and time frames for measurement. Imagine our surprise to learn that we were actually deeply aligned on the most important points! This realization helped us resolve many topics of previous dispute and to develop confidence in our conversational capacities for resolving new issues as they arose. The balance of the executive team was relieved to have us collaborate versus criticize, compete, or just tolerate each other, and not to feel as if they had to constantly choose sides. It was the beginning of a relationship built on mutual trust, respect, and safety.

Practice Opportunities: Listen Newly, Be Intentionally Slow to Understand

Open Up to Other Viewpoints

Make a list of about five topics in recent conversations where you had a different or conflicting point of view with another person.

1. Consider your instant point of view about each and make a note next to each topic.
2. Ask yourself, "Is it possible there are other valid perspectives?" Hint: The answer is always yes…there are many!

Have a *new* conversation about those topics with the people involved.

1. Turn your attention to understanding their perspectives.
2. Start by letting the other person know that you are committed to working things out and developing more effective ways of interacting with each other.
3. Make it clear that you are interested in their perspectives and in developing shared approaches that might be more powerful than either of you have created separately.

After the conversation, ask yourself:

- What happened when I considered other perspectives?
- How was the new conversation received?
- What part was hardest for me?
- What do I see happening next with each of the conversations?
- How do I feel about my participation in the conversation?
- What did I learn about this new approach to listening and about what the other person's view provided?

Operating Principle #3:

Take Myself Lightly

It's Not All About You...Stay in the Game

Taking myself lightly means trading my self-absorption for connecting with others...it is really not all about you! One of our workshop participants relates to this principle in this way: Don't make yourself more important than the situation.

Most one-to-one or group situations (unless you are in military combat) are not win-or-lose situations where you have to prove yourself or die. Today, even most sales and negotiation training programs have shifted their focus to win-win techniques and strategies. Generally your opinion or way of doing things is not necessarily the ultimate or only viable solution. Clinging, white knuckled, to your own point of view is a very self-absorbed, internally focused way to completely miss what is right in front of you. Many opportunities and solutions are available for those who look up and look out. Taking yourself lightly is a method to get outside yourself and back into the game at hand. It gets the focus off of you and back to the issue and to listening newly! Reminding yourself that a topic or situation probably isn't deadly allows everyone to relax a bit and remove some of the potentially unproductive emotions from the interaction, creating more connection and a safer atmosphere.

Lighten Up!

Taking yourself lightly also means you can lighten up on self-judgments, understanding that you are human and part of a bigger whole called the human race. By projecting an accepting and even self-deprecating attitude, you open up opportunities for others to contribute without feeling threatened. A light touch of well-placed and appropriate humor can clear the air, diffusing potential conflict and creating a safe atmosphere for dissent and discussion. The exception to this approach is the type of humor, or banter that occurs at another's expense. That approach diminishes others and creates an unsafe condition for productive conversation.

Make light of your own foibles, views (when appropriate), and situations in which you find yourself, and you'll find that everyone around you is more relaxed and open. This is an increasingly important leadership practice in times of unrelenting change, where "fear is everywhere" and dire financial and personal situations seem to rule the day.

One of our clients tells us that this is about personal humility. Taking yourself too seriously puts you in defense mode. It is not difficult to slip into a mind-set where defending your ego becomes more important than solving the problem. Then you are locked into your position and must defend it at risk of invalidating your ego. Letting go of your ego opens the door to taking a new and creative course of action.

Taking It Personally Has Consequences

> *Self-importance requires that one spend most of one's life offended by something or someone.*

> **Carlos Castaneda**–*Peruvian born American Author*

How can you reconcile the Essential Notion of Self-Generated Accountability and this Operating Principle, *Take Myself Lightly*? Can you stand with one foot planted in personal responsibility and the other in not taking things personally?

Don Miguel Ruiz, in his popular book *The Four Agreements*, considers this topic so important that the second of his four agreements is "Don't take *anything* personally." His writings support our Operating Principle in the following ways:

1. When you take something personally, you will most likely react defensively and be thrown instantly and automatically into survival mode.
2. Other people's statements and realities (that you have now taken personally) come from their own view of the world and their view of you–their own File Cabinet. It is not 'the truth' about you or the situation, it's just their view, to which they are entitled and to which they will most likely cling anyway.
3. When your opinions or perspectives are challenged, it is very common to react as if your opinions and perspectives *are* you and that you have been challenged. You have opinions and perspectives and they are *not* you!
4. By taking things personally, you set yourself up to suffer. The impact on you and the ripple effects on those around you are unhealthy.

Don't Take Others Lightly!

Many a true word is spoken in jest!

That doesn't mean that you take others lightly. This is about lightening up your own rigid opinions and concepts to create an opening for new learning. Humor at the expense of others can instantly diminish mutual trust, respect, and safety. Witty barbs generally indicate a lack of courage or the skill to deliver an authentic message. They shut down vulnerability, risk, and willingness to take responsibility. Consider the way you use humor. Does it lighten up the situation to allow for more creativity or is it a veiled complaint disguised in humor?

Survival Brain Thinking

The more intense your emotions, the more distorted your perception.

John J. Scherer—*Five Questions that Change Everything: Life Lessons at Work*

For intensely serious issues, the faculty most needed is your ability to be fully present and think creatively. Neither of these faculties is easy or even possible when you are in life-or-death, survival brain thinking. Grasping the fundamentals of survival brain thinking and the consequences on your emotions, behavior, and interactions is fundamental to successfully mastering the principles in this book. While the brain activity involved and how it impacts you are fairly easy to describe and understand, learning to self-diagnose when you are "in it," let alone learning to free yourself and employ more effective practices in your interactions, is a lifetime discipline. The "survival brain" is the part of your brain that is activated when you are under stress and focuses your reactions in a fight, flight, freeze, or appease mode. While often problematic in conversations, it is an important part of our anatomy, since the design is to keep us safe from physical threats.

◇◆◇

I once stepped off the curb in London after having looked the wrong way and jumped back just in time to avoid being struck by a taxi…without my survival brain I might not have survived!

John Gray—*Founder, Glen Ivy Hot Springs, Inc., Corona, California, and Principal, Voelker Gray Design, Irvine, California*

◇◆◇

When you are committed to fruitful conversations with others, it is essential to know that the survival brain can't tell the difference between a physical threat to survival and a threat in language. While you seldom need your survival brain for physical safety in the office, it is triggered much too often as a result of comments and expressions you experience from others. To make matters worse, you are unlikely to know in advance when your language occurs as a threat to another person.

> Remember the children's rhyme about "sticks and stones"? It is true that words, while perhaps painful or upsetting, are not physically deadly. Unfortunately, since your survival brain cannot tell the difference between a physical threat and a threat in language, the mental, emotional, and physical reactions are very similar.

There's no perspective available in the survival brain because that attribute resides in another, contextual part of your brain. Regarding a situation as "life or death" drops you into that stupid, limited reactive brain and you start to roar or run, lash out, get quiet (whatever your default response), and generally let emotions reign. For some, "life or death" reactions show up as fearful avoidance of conversations, believing, "I might die if I tell them *that*." Taking yourself lightly helps prevent that dinosaur-like or turtle-like response, so you can move from the Emotional Zone of Upset and Distress into the Learning Zone where communications and creative ideas can flow.

As you learn to spot when you are triggered and in the Distress-Upset Zone where your survival brain dominates, you can intervene in your distress by taking that reaction lightly as well. There is nothing wrong with you because you have upsetting survival brain reactions. As far as we know, you won't ever get to a place in life where you don't have them. The most valuable question to ask yourself is, "How fast can I spot my survival brain reaction, let go of it, and get back to being present?"

A Self-Management Practice

When there is an important or "heavy" issue being dealt with, it is probably inappropriate to inject humor. However, you can still "lighten up" by being sure that you have cleared your emotions around the issue before you enter into a conversation. Sharing how upset you have been is very different than talking while you are upset. Take a moment to breathe, get present, identify the current conditions of your situation, separate your emotions from it, and cool down. Your moderated response is much less likely to create distress and upset in others and will help keep the overall mood open and relaxed.

Breathe. Fear and oxygen cannot occupy the same space.

Amrit Desai–*a pioneer of yoga in the West*

Separating your emotions from the issue does not mean to ignore, invalidate, or judge it. It really means to separate, i.e., "this happened *and* I feel this way." To effectively connect with others about your observation, it is essential to start your share with something like "I realize that I had a very strong reaction to the conversation we just had and lost my perspective." A statement like "you made me very upset when you said..." will be perceived as an attack, not an opening for connection and understanding. In the Practical Applications— Section Five, see "From Upset to Productivity–Uncovering and Speaking Commitment" for more discussion about emotional barriers, upsets, fears, and worries and how to work through them to productivity.

Why is Taking Myself Lightly Important?

When you are intensely focused and locked on to your own point of view or your own unproductive emotions, you are unavailable for collaboration. Learn to step up to a higher level of thinking and to look outward to include everything around you. This critical leadership skill is a means to bring you present and back in the game. An appropriate level of lightheartedness can lift a conversation to a level where participation and creativity flourish. Taking yourself lightly helps make sure you keep focused on the Yonder Star rather than being derailed into your own or another's personal drama.

What Difference Does It Make?

In an environment where distress, defensiveness, and unproductive emotions can be quickly cleared, everyone can concentrate on the tasks at hand to fulfill the Yonder Star. The environment is safer and more productive, and mutual trust and respect build. Creativity increases, as people are more likely to speak out and contribute ideas with less fear of ridicule or teasing. You earn a reputation as someone who makes it easy for people to talk, no matter how tough the issue, since you are able to interject lightness and perspective into what otherwise could be a tense and uncomfortable situation.

When Taking Myself Lightly Is Missing:

- You take yourself or the process too seriously or too intensely, losing perspective.

- You produce sarcasm, witty barbs, or comments made at another's expense, which tend to create an unsafe space and shut down those around you.

- You accuse other people of not being as committed or as interested as you are.

- When a critical or negative remark is made, you react from your survival brain with fight, flight, freeze, or appease behavior, depending on your own default responses.

- Other participants in the discussion are stifled in their desire to have a productive conversation.

When This Principle Is in Play:

- You have the ability, even in intense situations, to take a breath, relax, and actually lighten up.

- When the mood becomes tense, you are skilled at offering a lighter view or interpretation of the circumstances.

- If you get emotionally triggered after something is said, you catch yourself, acknowledge being triggered, and do what it takes to get back on an emotionally even keel before continuing the conversation.

- If you make an error or misstate something, you are able to openly admit it and reflect lightly (distinct from flippantly) on the cause.

- You can forgive yourself for your mistakes and use them as a forward-facing learning opportunity.

Case Study: Take Myself Lightly

Dwight—Staying Sane in a Storm

My first boss gave me one of my best illustrations of taking a situation lightly. I was fresh out of graduate school and had joined a company where one man was the sole owner. Prior to my joining this company, it had gotten into financial difficulties, and at this point we were at the brink of failing and closing the company. My boss stood to lose everything, and the bank that had loaned the company money would be left with one of its largest losses ever.

It was the end of the line, "game over" time. So what did my boss do? He took us to lunch at a Polynesian restaurant to discuss the situation and see what could be done. He was in a happy, uplifting mood, joking around about golf and life during the meal. At the end, little fortune cookies were placed on the table. "Ah, gentlemen," he said with a grin, "now we'll do some strategic planning." His course of action: open the cookies to see what to do to assure staying in business that week.

He was demonstrating how we could each get off the deep end of serious and out of our survival brains. We were scared to death—and he was concerned about keeping our creative juices flowing. He knew that the most important thing we could do was to create effective ideas and the courage to execute them, rather than fall prey to knee-jerk responses that wouldn't get us anywhere. His lightness was catching and, after a while, we all began to be playful with each other in the face of constant dire threats to our firm's survival. We eventually paid the bank back 100 percent of our loans and all interest due, and the company went on to be a viable player in our market.

Case Study: Take Myself Lightly

A Knife Through the Heart

Jim was in charge of manufacturing, and had a good working relationship with his boss, Dan. One month-end there was a *huge* surprise gap in total shipments compared to projections and the shortfall created a serious problem. Jim and Dan had intense conversations about what happened and how to prevent such a surprise in the future, and Jim thought they'd worked it all out.

One afternoon after work, a group from the manufacturing division and some people from upper management joined in the parking lot to shoot baskets before they headed home. "I thought we had it worked out," Jim said, "but during the basketball game, when I dribbled down the court, faked, stumbled, and missed my shot, my boss said, 'Ha, that looked like your stumble in missing the shipment projections last month!' There was dead silence on the court, then nervous laughter and Dan said, 'Come on, I was just kidding!' " Dan had used sarcasm, a witty barb, probably more out of habit than a purposeful intent to damage. However, everyone who heard the comment, while relieved that he or she was not the brunt of the humor, became more cautious and distrustful.

Jim had another conversation with Dan—using "I" statements—where they were able to validate that part of their relationship and interactions where humor did lighten up tough conversations and bring forth creativity—*and* confront the times and places where humor was destructive, directed at others, or masked real issues. They made a pact to mutually support each other in this area shared it with the entire staff at their next meeting. While there was a background feeling of "wait and see," the staff was impressed with the transparency demonstrated by Jim and Dan, their commitment to improve the productivity of their conversations, and the way they both took responsibility for the impact and ripple effect of their comments.

Practice Opportunities:
Take Myself Lightly

Catching Survival Brain Mode

1. List five situations where you get frustrated, overly intense, impatient, or express unproductive emotions that take you out of the game.
2. Create a simple mantra—a brain assignment—to intervene in your unproductive mode. Keep it short and easy to remember. For example:

   - "What's the opportunity for leadership here?"
   - "Get a grip and lighten up!"
   - "OK, it's not all about me—focus 'up and out,'" or
   - "What's the bigger picture here?"

3. Make notes about how this new brain assignment might change your approach to the situations, and the outcomes.
4. The next time you are in an intensive or unpleasant situation, proactively catch yourself, exhale slowly, pull out the mantra, and use it.

Afterward, ask yourself:

- What situations are most difficult for me to catch myself in survival brain mode?
- What happened when I caught myself and used my mantra?
- How did it change the interaction?
- What did I learn about this approach to lightening up?

Advanced Practice Opportunity: Take Myself Lightly

Sarcasm to Clarity

There really is no such thing as "just a joke" when it is at someone else's expense. It carries a message, especially coming from someone in a leadership position. Make a list of situations you can recall where you did this, so that you are really aware of them. One of our clients told us that he started noticing where he said (or even thought), "Aw, shucks, we were just joking around and having a good time," and would use his own statement as a mental trigger to consider what behaviors or points of view he was justifying. Are there themes to notice about the times you use humor inappropriately? Do you use it as an attack or a defense mechanism? Or are you using humor to dismiss or diminish another or to simply to avoid difficult topics? *The next time you reach for the sarcasm, do the following:*

1. Stop in midsentence.
2. Put your mind in reverse, back up, and apologize.
3. Reframe what you have to say without the barbs.

After that reframed conversation, ask yourself:

- What happened when I did this? How did others receive it?
- What difference did it make to creating a safe and respectful environment?
- What did I learn about myself...about eliminating sarcasm...about the Operating Principle?
- How did it open up opportunities for me in my interactions?
- Who could mentor me in this area?

Section Three:
Reality Check

The difference between your aspirations—your Yonder Star—and the current condition in which you find yourself creates a gap to fulfill with action. Your actions will be most productive if you design them based on a clear picture of your starting point. To do so requires being present to your circumstances, the drivers of those circumstances, the rate of change going on around you, and as many dimensions of the current condition as possible.

The three Operating Principles presented in the previous section of this book provide access to being present, listening newly, and taking yourself lightly. These are essential prerequisites for clarity on the situation *in which you find yourself*. In this section, we'll ask you to consider how some of your common labels such as "wrong" and "broken" create screens or barriers to that clarity and to your ability to engage others in a collaborative process. We'll also tackle definitions for "truth" and "confront" that enhance your ability to create a context or environment of mutual trust, respect, and safety for your conversations.

Integrating the Operating Principles in this section will give you the ability to see and speak about the way that it is and the way that it isn't (the present) rather than be stuck in how it should have been or how you wanted it to be (the past). People in the military refer to this description of current conditions as "ground truth" rather than how the situation was supposed to be when the mission was planned. These three Operating Principles dig deeply into the automatic and unconscious thinking that prevents or distorts your grasp of the way that it is and isn't.

Naming Reality—the Current Conditions

Just as one of the most important first steps in a journey involves knowing your ultimate destination, a critical aspect of powerfully embarking on your quest for your Yonder Star is accurately identifying the ground truth of your starting point.

The past is not exactly your current reality, and neither are your opinions about it. To bring yourself present to the reality before you, ask and answer: "What exactly am I dealing with here?" Observe the way that it is and the way that it isn't without adding or detracting from it. If you cannot accurately assess the current condition, particularly in the human dimension, then your starting point and your picture of what it will take to get to your goal will be distorted and inadequate at best.

A simple analogy is entering a destination into your GPS or navigation system. Without an accurate starting point, the system is of no use. Once it connects to a satellite link and identified your current location, it can successfully map out the route to your destination based on the two points and any additional criteria you may have entered. When the navigational system reports "lost satellite connection," it has lost the ability to track and update your current position. The system can no longer give you a route until location data is again available.

The process of looking back from your fulfilled Yonder Star to identify what's missing in your current reality and then using the gap you have identified as your guide to getting into action in the most powerful way may seem like a relatively simple concept. Unfortunately, identifying your current reality may not be as easy as seems. It really requires that you realize and begin to relate to what you have been calling "the real world" as only *your own* interpretations and story, framed and filtered by your self-concept and worldview.

Dueling Realities—Now What?

Chris Argyris, an American business theorist and professor emeritus from Harvard Business School, is known for his work in the area of "Learning Organizations." His concept of Action Science studies how human beings design their actions in difficult situations. His Ladder of Inference (http://www.systems-thinking.org/loi/loi.htm) has been widely studied and used extensively to support other people's work, including in Peter Senge's book *The Fifth Discipline: The Art and Practice of the Learning Organization*. In the Ladder of Inference, Argyris models how we often short-circuit reality by our tendency to select data that reinforce and support our own beliefs and experiences. In this way it becomes an internally referencing circuit that shortcuts the consideration of new data from outside our internal loop.

From the early 1800s to present day, scholars and scientists have been studying *Confirmation Bias, Priming Effect, Power of Expectation* and *Schema Theory* which are represented simply in the following quote:

◇◇◇

The moment a person forms a theory; his imagination sees in every object only the traits which favor that theory.

Thomas Jefferson–*Third President of the United States* and principal author of *The Declaration of Independence*

◇◇◇

This contrast between your reality and someone else's reality is what usually causes friction in conversations and often devolves to a dueling File Cabinet battle over who is right.

Dueling File Cabinets
Convince and Convert Mode

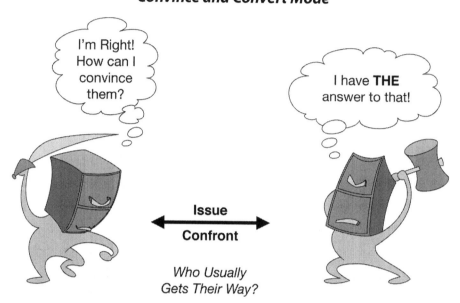

Instead, consider that differing perspectives provide excellent grounds for exploration and learning. Let differences be a trigger for your curiosity mode versus your dueling mode. Be willing to allow that your perceptions and ideas are a subset of a larger group of perceptions and ideas. The basis for truly effective problem solving lies in acknowledging and appreciating the larger set and working toward a shared reality that allows all participants to align on the most effective actions to fulfill the Yonder Star.

If you refuse to acknowledge other realities, you get stuck in your own reality and develop ways to ignore or resist others' viewpoints. You pull up old notions and treat them as if they still apply (like expecting Sally to add nothing new to the conversation because, in your view, she's been a useless contributor in the past), or you adamantly hold to your vision as the only acceptable one. Others naturally resist, either openly or passively. Fight, flight, freeze, and appease begin to define the conversation.

My Ideas are a Subset of All Ideas

Considering different yet valid and valuable "realities" will increase velocity and success in working with others to achieve higher productivity. Most importantly, by sorting out the way that it is and the way that it isn't, it is easier to confront and deal with the issues that are usually avoided as being "too difficult." You can face head-on the stuff that everyone has been tiptoeing around. Typical examples of such topics are those that are normally deferred until the meeting in the restroom at the break or in the bar and those things you would never take up directly with a boss or colleague.

Now it's time to explore the principles that give you new capacities to be more fully present to the way that it is and the way that it isn't. Explore and integrate the following three Operating Principles, and practice, practice, practice.

Operating Principle #4:

Declare There is Nothing Wrong or Broken *Here and Now*

"There is nothing either good or bad, but thinking makes it so."

William Shakespeare–*Act 2, Scene 2 of Hamlet*

There are three key components involved in this operating principle; *Declare, "Wrong,"* and the *Present* moment. Remember we often use different words, phrasing, or terminology to evoke (or provoke) new, productive ways of thinking and relating. Some readers may struggle with this principle at first. If you are one who does, stay with it, as we've found that this single Operating Principle, while challenging at first, has created big openings for many clients to increase their collaborative effectiveness.

Declarations

Declaration: The formal announcement of the beginning of a state or condition. Origin: late Middle English, from Latin declarare, "make quite clear."

Creative Acts in Language

The first aspect of this Operating Principle to consider is our use of the word *Declare*—a creative act in language. Human beings are, you are, creating your own world minute by minute through declarations. Declarations are an element we use to bring things into existence, to create new parts of the game of life. They are statements that often have little or no basis in current facts or historical evidence and with little to no indication that they are even possible.

◇◇◇

"We hold these truths to be self-evident, that all men are created equal, that they are endowed by their Creator with certain unalienable Rights, that among these are Life, Liberty and the pursuit of Happiness."

Excerpt from the Unanimous Declaration of the Thirteen United States of America

◇◇◇

One of the easiest examples illustrating this point is the U.S. Declaration of Independence. With that document, a very small group of bold individuals put into language their shared commitment and launched a new country with new values and beliefs that had little precedent in history and little agreement in the paradigm of the world at the time. Yet a powerful, evolving nation was birthed that prides itself in valuing human life, liberty, and the pursuit of happiness. This shared declaration was paired with a tremendous amount of courage and commitment. They pledged their lives, their fortunes, and their sacred honor. That creation is still growing and evolving to this day, clearly illustrating the power and sustainability of a declaration.

Many of the statements that you make each day are declarations, and yet you don't necessarily recognize them as such. Nevertheless, they are still extremely powerful in shaping your life, your views, and your progress (or lack thereof) in fulfilling your Yonder Star. Often simple and seemingly unimportant or throwaway statements create your reality. Contrast "I am going to have a great vacation" with "I'm not any good at math." Both create realities for you, albeit very different ones. The first time you say them (whether out loud or to yourself) they launch you on a path. As you repeat them, they reinforce a pattern recognition formula that filters what you subsequently see and hear. In other words they create your mental contextual framework that defines what content you can ever see or hear. They shape your mind-set, thought process, decision making, reality, your self-concept, and worldview, and the range of outcomes that are available to you, whether you realize it or not.

Beware of "Wanna-be" Language

It is useful to briefly examine common statements that masquerade as declarations and yet do not create powerful new realities. Some common examples are "we really *should* do that project," "I *need* to lose weight,"' "I *want* to start exercising," "wouldn't it *be nice if* we had more resources," "*hopefully* we will..." and the classic "I'm *trying* to..." These statements and many like them are merely verbal pollution that almost never cause any meaningful actions or results. It's wimpy "wanna-be" language, lacking real commitment. Pay attention when such phrases come out of your mouth (or occur in your thinking) and get rigorous with yourself. Are you going to or not? Remember Yoda's famous line from the movie *The Emperor Strikes Back*, Episode V of the *Star Wars* series: "Do, or do not, there is no try!" Give up using such language and be vigilant about letting those around you use it with you. It is too easy to allow such a statement to be mistaken for promised action. Inaction, failure, and disappointment will almost certainly follow.

What's Wrong with "Wrong"?

> *The difference between a free person and one without freedom is not bars or doors, but the extent to which they are able to choose their state of mind.*

> **Anonymous**

Declarations Create Context that Shape and Direct Action

What context does the declaration "wrong" create for your interactions? Where does it turn your focus or the focus of others? What path does it choose for you?

So much of what gets discussed, particularly on the airwaves, is how things have gone wrong—our economy, our government, our banks, our schools, and pretty much everything else. Being embroiled in this state of "wrong" keeps many people from breaking free of their interpretation of the conditions in their lives so that they can get to work on coming up with new ways of dealing with their real challenges.

We are in no way proposing a new moral code, or lack of one, or saying that this Operating Principle has universal application. It is not something to be believed. It is an alternative perspective from which to view your situation and to design alternative strategies and actions. It is especially valuable for conversations where creativity, free and open exchange, and the best possible outcomes are the most valuable elements of the conversation. Remember, the Operating Principles are to be invoked when you are committed to interacting and getting to work with others with the highest productivity possible. Can you choose your mind-set? Whether you are solving problems or generating creative new ideas, making the declaration, "There is nothing wrong or broken *here and now*" will put your mind into a present, open, receptive, and supportive mode. Practice this principle and, when you get some facility with it, notice the different results you are experiencing.

A Past-Based Label that Provokes Defense

> *What you need to know about the past is that no matter what has happened, it has all worked together to bring you to this very moment. And this is the moment you can choose to make everything new. Right Now.*

> **Anonymous**

"Wrong" is a label generated in *your* mind from *your* point of view. This declarative label sets your mind up in a way that generally drives your thought processes and conversations down the unproductive lower line in the Leadership Choice Point versus taking it up the upper line toward the Yonder Star. Marilee Adams, PhD, in her book *Change*

Your Questions, Change Your Life, calls it the "judger path" versus the "learner path."

It relates to something that has happened in the past, a place where nothing can be done or undone. It sends others to their File Cabinet for past-based justifications, shifts the focus generally backward instead of forward, and tends to mask the real issues and challenges.

"Wrong" is often an emotionally charged judgment that produces an impotent, defensive explanation. It is also a loaded term, generally implying that some person is to blame. The consequence is that other participants in the conversation often take the allegation personally and become defensive and protective. It disconnects people from each other and from the Yonder Star as the priority turns to self-preservation above all.

Many times the reason a group of people meet is to resolve a problem or find a solution for something that is not working as planned. It is easy for the perspective "wrong" or "broken" to hang over everything. That raises the strong likelihood of attack-defend, hide out or cover up, appease, or "get-it-over-with" behavior on at least someone's part, right when creative problem solving is what's needed most.

Initiating a conversation blame-free allows group members to focus on identifying mutually observable facts as the starting point for productive collaboration. By thinking and speaking from this declaration, you acknowledge that the facts are simply the facts without negative connotations or meanings read into the situation. Instead of having people running off to build a protective case for themselves or wasting time investigating something that can't be changed in the past, they are present and engaged in seeking a productive way forward together.

Don't Should on Me!

A word that often signals wrong and blame is the word "should." When you are thinking or saying a phrase that involves "should," for example, "I should lose weight" or "I should speak up more at meetings," experiment with substituting the word "could." "Should" is a term loaded with judgment, blame, sacrifice, and guilt. It carries no commitment with it, and it creates a limited set of solutions. "Could" is a forward-facing term, opening up possibilities and multiple solutions. It calls on you to make a choice. Are you going to go for it or not? Wouldn't you rather think "I *could* lose weight," which sets your mind working on solutions to that gap? Aren't you more inspired and motivated by your goal than having your mind work on all the different ways to generate self-blame?

When you replace "should" with "could" in conversations with others, they'll hear your comment as a question, input, or a recommendation. It sets the other person up to choose freely for him or herself versus reacting to a judgment or condemnation they hear from you. For example, "You should talk to her about that!" changed to "You could talk to her about that." Check for more examples in the Practical Applications— Section Five at the end of the book.

> Eliminate "should" from your vocabulary (and your mind-set) and then notice how interactions ease up around you. You may even discover that people are more interested in your input. This is definitely a principle to try at home with your teenagers or significant other!

Use Your Words, People, Use Your Words!

As we've said, facilitating movement toward fulfilling your Yonder Star requires an *accurate* assessment of the current condition. In addition to provoking defense when using "wrong" as a label, it is also a dead-end explanation. It truncates any constructive action and obscures the reality of the situation. As a descriptive label, "wrong" just isn't very helpful. When you label a situation as "wrong," notice how there is no new creative action identified.

Using "wrong" rather than accurately describing what you see as missing, "out of specification," or present when it doesn't belong is analogous to being a very young child with wants. When young children have only learned a few words and have not yet made the switch to using their words to describe what they want or what is distressful to them, a frustrated parent may say, "Use your words, Johnny, use your words. Tell me what's bothering you." While parents could venture a guess as to what is troubling their child, it seems much more productive to hear the child use his or her words to tell them. We have made the same request to clients whose discussion was stuck using "wrong" to describe the issue: "Use your words, people, use your words." Most professions have a much larger and more precise vocabulary to describe a problem than just "it's wrong." See the Case Study at the end of this chapter: *In Spec or Not in Spec.*

A Self-Management Practice

If you use the words "I agree" or "I disagree" very frequently, you are unwittingly in right/wrong and attack mode. When you disagree it means you have checked your File Cabinet records and can't find any that match or you don't like the matches you did find, so you say, "I disagree." Generally the other person now has to defend what he or she has said, and you are now in a dueling File Cabinet, convince-and-convert mode. Instead, catch yourself when you are about to disagree and say: "My File Cabinet records don't match yours"—OK, well, not exactly! Use "I" statements and try out, "I see it quite differently; would you help me understand your view?" Notice how the interaction flows and how differences from your past experience, while valid, don't have to damage this interaction.

Consider judicious use of the phrase "I agree" as well and limit it to times in a conversation when choices are being made rather than during creative, explorative phases. What "I agree" really means is, "I have checked my File Cabinet records and found a match." Does that make it the best solution just because your File Cabinet records match? Consider the impact of the use of "I agree" in a group setting. While you may not mean to create mental havoc in your group, when you say "I agree with you, Sally," everyone else who has put forth a suggestion goes straight into their heads to ask something like, "Does that mean he doesn't agree with me?" and on down an unproductive bunny trail. Their thought processes have been diverted from the issue at hand since self-preservation is a powerful motivation!

As a leader, be wary of using "agree" or "disagree." If it is a habit of yours, you will notice that people around you focus their time and energy on bringing forth ideas that you will agree with and avoiding saying things with which you will disagree. That is how you have trained them! If all you ever hear are solutions and recommendations that match your own File Cabinet records, your options will be severely limited, and your access to anything creative or truly new will be nil.

Mind the Gap

> *'Mind the Gap' is a standard warning to train passengers regarding the sometimes-significant gap between the train door and the station platform in the London Underground transit system. 'Mind the Gap' is painted in capitals at the edge of such platforms and is also an announcement played when trains arrive.*

The same warning is true regarding focus for your energy and attention. The most productive focus is on the gap between current conditions and your Yonder Star. When you get caught up in judgment or past-based thinking, you have diverted your focus away from that gap.

In the movie *Apollo 13*, Ed Harris, as Gene Krantz, reminds everyone, "Let's work the problem, people!" In one of our client companies several of the directors now invoke, "Yonder Star, people, Yonder Star" as their version of Ed Harris' admonition.

A Self-Management Practice

Catch Yourself in "Convince and Convert" Mode

"Wrong" as a concept can pop up in your thinking in various ways. It is a label driven by judgments and conclusions that are a function of your instant, automatic, and largely unexamined reactions, which are in turn shaped by the records stored in your mental File Cabinet. Anything that does not match your own File Cabinet contents can occur to you as wrong, and then you may work hard, using all of your ammunition if necessary, to convince others that the contents of your File Cabinet are right. We call that "convince and convert mode."

Instead, use those automatic, internal voice comments (or external voice if they have already come out of your mouth) as a diagnostic to trigger a choice point for yourself. Develop the patience and skills to self-observe—to listen to your own thoughts and the words coming out of your mouth. You will not be able to intervene the way a coach might intervene in your pattern of thought unless you pay attention to your thoughts and comments, particularly when you don't like the sound of them. Rather than hastily defending your statement with "I didn't mean it that way," own up to the fact that your words can give you guidance to your unexamined automatic thoughts. These are areas where you can work on catching your judgment mind-set, and consciously shift to a curious, learner mind-set. Once you've become able

> to self-observe, stop, and reframe your mind-set to curiosity, you are on the road to effective self-coaching! See the Practical Application—Section Five: *Unmasking the Issue—Reframing "Wrong"* for useful examples.

Today, common business approaches to dealing with problems and errors include "root cause analysis" and "project review." In many cases when an incident occurs, everyone runs off to accomplish one or both of these, looking for ways to "right the wrong." Productive investigations and analysis will occur if the approach starts with asking, "What happened?" and explores multiple vantage points. Often such a conversation can simply be a discussion of what worked and what didn't work. On the other hand, if the inquiry starts from right/wrong, the result will most often be a situation where people are defensive, afraid to speak up and tell the truth, so little, if any, new learning takes place.

> *A Pitfall to Watch For*
>
> Sometimes when people haven't fully developed their understanding of the value and application of this principle, they use it as a shield to deflect blame or avoid further discussion of tough issues. In the face of a breakdown, missed deadline, or broken promise, their first quick-response words might be, "Remember, there is nothing wrong or broken here" (usually said while holding their hands up in front of themselves). While this declaration creates a powerful context for addressing issues, subverting the intent and using it as a shield has the opposite effect.

Enter into a conversation or meeting with the mind-set that the issue or situation you are dealing with is *not* wrong or broken, rather, "It is what it is and is not what it is not, so let's learn what we can." This starting point allows you to loosen your past's grip, get clear about the conditions of the current situation, and open yourself to new possibilities. You will be freed up, and your openness to possibility will shape the mood to "What is next from here?" or simply "OK, now what?" Application of this upgrade to your mental software creates a vacuum or opening that calls forth creativity, produces an immediate attitude adjustment, and keeps the focus on "real issues." Your brain will want to know what to work on if nothing is wrong. Aim it at the Yonder Star, fill in the current situation and any added search criteria, and let it get busy on closing the gap.

If you integrate the principles of Self-Generated Accountability discussed in Section Two with declaring "nothing wrong or broken," you will soon be comfortable openly stepping up, engaging with others and creating new solutions. You will find new freedom to explore rather than being run by a concept that keeps you stuck in the past, feeling like a victim, hunting for who to blame, or defending your accusatory or judging mind-set.

Presence— *Here and Now*

> *If you want to know your past, look at your current situation; if you want to know about your future, look at your current actions.*

Chinese Proverb

The third aspect of this Operating Principle is presence, invoked by the last three words, "here and now." These words have been italicized in the statement of the principle specifically to draw special attention to the important role presence plays in your ability to come from a problem-solving, learner's mind-set. *Here and now* means in this conversation *right now,* in this meeting *right now.* Right here, right now, you are bringing yourself present to the current conditions. You are bringing an explorer's listening in such a way that you are contributing to clarity and forward movement. You are not stuck in past-based "what ifs," "if onlys," or fear-based "now we'll never..." or "this makes it impossible now to..."

Give up trying to create a better past!

You can release any need to dwell in the past because the evidence of the past is in your present. The way to impact your future is to connect to your Yonder Star in the present, discover the gap, and design new strategies and actions to begin closing the gap. Notice that your Yonder Star lives in the present, and every step of the strategies and actions will always be carried out in the present!

Why Is It Important to Declare There is Nothing Wrong or Broken, Here and Now?

Your ability to move forward quickly in the face of distressing circumstances is a critical leadership practice for a fast-paced, ever-changing environment. You can't afford the friction and waste that are generated by unthinking, defense-provoking, nondescriptive labels. Since your thoughts explode into your brain with breakneck speed, this declaration causes an instant intervention in your unproductive thought context. In addition to limiting your own creative capacities when you are in a judging mind-set, your thoughts show up in your speaking, listening and body language. To be a person around whom issues can be raised and resolved productively your ability to be present to the circumstances and to facilitate creativity and collaboration are essential leadership capacities.

What Difference Does It Make?

It immediately evokes a team mentality, where everyone is looking for the most accurate perception of the current situation and exploring for clarity on what the *is* really is. It sets up an open inquiry (without blame or recrimination) and the most creative ways to deal with the issue at hand. Making this powerful declaration immediately reframes the situation you find yourself in, making it easier to look for solutions that are compatible with fulfilling your Yonder Star. By removing blame or judgment, you can create a safe environment where self protecting activities no longer occur, Self-Generated Accountability flourishes, and participants are freed up to pursue a common goal. By making this declaration, you improve your ability to be present, quickly access mutually observable facts, and get to work on solutions.

When the Declaration 'There Is Nothing Wrong or Broken Here and Now' Is Missing:

- The focus is no longer on the Yonder Star or the gap; it is on staying clear of blame.

- You dwell on the past; "should-ing" on others and wasting time telling others how you thought it was a bad idea in the first place.

- You are blind to nuance and subtleties.

- You miss opportunities to learn from the situation or from others.

- Unproductive emotions abound, and lots of people get caught up in the drama.

- Team members scurry back to their offices and lay low.

When This Principle Is in Play:

- You are able to listen newly and be present.

- You are catching yourself in judgment and shifting to curiosity and learning.

- You can talk about emotions rather than speaking while in your emotions.

- You are exploring the circumstances as a situation report with clear data.

- Your focus is Vision-Focused, on the Yonder Star.

- The prevailing attitude is, "What are we really dealing with? Where are we headed? What is missing? What is next?"

- "Should" is gone from your vocabulary.

Case Study: Declare There is Nothing Wrong or Broken *Here and Now*

In Spec or Not in Spec?

When presenting this Principle during one of our Productive Interactions courses, a quality engineer named Mark said, "Come on…this is a manufacturing firm…there is stuff that just gets made wrong sometimes."

I asked Mark where in his engineering studies he encountered the topic "When Stuff Gets Made *Wrong*." What does the label "wrong" really tell us? What specific action can we move forward with as a result of that label? Isn't it more accurate, and actionable, to label it as "in spec" or "not in spec"? For example "This part is .08 mm shorter than spec, or the point is stubbed versus pointed…or however you describe variances?"

Allison shared that his statement "this part is made wrong" negatively impacts her willingness to help resolve the issue. She shared that she usually gets defensive. Mark realized that the way he had been interacting with people was generating the exact defense response he said he wished he didn't have to deal with. His eyes were sparkling as if he had just come upon a magic bullet for realizing his intentions. What he really wanted was to figure out what happened, fix it, make sure it doesn't happen again, make the customer happy, and make it as easy as possible to be accurate in the manufacturing process (his Yonder Star). Allison realized that her part in the unproductive interactions was her instant and automatic defense and that she really shared the same Yonder Star with Mark. They saw that they could work together to accomplish it rather than interact as adversaries.

The entire group generated the shared Yonder Star of customer satisfaction and delivering quality products through a reliable process. In the process, they realized that they were all on the same team rather than departmental silos competing for credit or transferring blame.

125

Practice Opportunities: Declare There is Nothing Wrong or Broken *Here and Now*

Learn to Reframe Productively

1. Draw three columns on a blank piece of paper and label them "Name," "Wrong," and "Reframe." In the first "Name" column, list a few issues, situations, or names of people that you currently consider to be "wrong" or "broken." In the second column, make notes on what you consider to be "wrong" about that person or situation.

2. Before you fill in the third column, assess the impact or consequences of "wrong" as your description of the situation. Does it fall into one of these categories?

   a. dead-end label that disguises the issue
   b. judgment or attack that will probably induce defense
   c. directed at a person versus focused on the issue to be resolved

3. To fill in the third column, labeled "Reframe," restate your observation in one of the following four ways:

   - *Dead-end label:* Shift to wording that is more specific, accurate, descriptive, and actionable.
   - *Judgment/Attack:* Shift to questions you that would help clarify the current condition or help you understand the other person's perspective.
   - *Judgment/Attack:* Shift to a calm, descriptive training conversation.
   - *Directed at a Person:* Identify the issue separate from the person.

Read over your results, examining how your restatements offer a new perspective on the situation, and continue to practice incorporating these types of reframing statements in your conversations and interactions. Most importantly consider what shift in mind-set is required. Are you "free" enough of your File Cabinet to choose a productive perspective?

For specific suggestions on how to reframe your mind-set and resultant wording, check the Practical Application: *Unmasking the Issue—Reframing "Wrong"*.

Operating Principle #5:

Explore *truths*: Mine, Theirs, and Ours

In the introduction to this section of the book, we looked at the whole notion of "reality," how it fits in the context of Vision-Focused Leadership, the value of considering differing realities, and the impact being present has on effective collaboration. As we examine this Operating Principle, *Explore truths: Mine, Theirs, and Ours*, we will take the discussion to the next level, which involves the search for shared reality. Approaching your exploration with a curiosity mind-set will give you a valuable way of listening and speaking with which to conduct that search.

We format the word *truths* in this Operating Principle purposefully with a small "t" to indicate a shift from considering your own version of reality—or the situation at hand—as absolute truth, to acknowledging that what you view as truth may only be your own perspective. We placed an "s" at the end to emphasize two points: that there are a number of your own viewpoints you consider to be *The Truth* and that there are other perspectives that other people hold as their truths. Exploring your own truths is listed *first* in the principle and points to the critical prerequisite of being willing to question your own long-held notions and beliefs before you engage with another person or a group to explore their perspectives. As you progress to exploring with others, practice prior Operating Principles so that your exploration does not occur as a deposition or interrogation, which would almost certainly result in defense rather than exploration.

OK, What Exactly Is "truth"?

Is it what you see, say, or think...or is it my version, if it differs from yours? There are many differing yet coexisting versions of "the way things are." "Version" is defined as "an account of a matter from a particular person's point of view." The more diversity in your group, the more this business of "truth" can occur as a challenge. Alternatively, it can be viewed as an opportunity to be mined.

If you and the people with whom you are engaged are willing to dance with the infinite potential dimensions of "truth," you will have the opportunity to actively explore all perspectives, find common ground, and design creative solutions to your challenges. In fact, you'll probably discard the word "truth" very soon or substitute the word "perspective". We purposefully use the word "truth" in this Operating Principle to provoke your consideration of how often and unconsciously you use your own File Cabinet contents as if they are *The Truth*, or at least the only version that is important or valid.

◇◇◇

Life does not consist mainly, or even largely, of facts and happenings. It consists mainly of the storm of thought that is forever flowing through one's head.

Mark Twain–*American Author and Humorist*

◇◇◇

Exploring My "truths"

One of our colleagues considers this process as "weeding the garden of my perceptions, opinions, and judgments to be fully present to reality." Having *the* answer stops your learning. Acknowledging that the world doesn't always operate strictly according to your perceptions can be a definite cage-rattler. You are being asked to own and contribute your own truth and at the same time accept that you can learn something different from the world you know by listening to other truths.

Notice when you are working hard in a conversation to convince others of your perspective and convert them to your point of view. There is probably a firmly held truth right under the surface. Since you don't have a monopoly on reality and neither does anyone else, see if you are willing to loosen your grip on your view. Opening up your own position is one of the quickest ways to get others to soften theirs so you can jointly get on with creating a shared truth.

When I nail one of my cherished beliefs to the floor...I can no longer deepen its meaning, nor release it when it does not serve my spirit.

John Konstanturos–*Founder, Continuous Renewal. Consulting and training programs for senior executives.*

Our mind's habitual way of acquiring a new piece of information is to encounter it, check to see if it agrees or disagrees with our existing File Cabinet data, give it a label for easy retrieval according to our own interpretation of it, and store it for future use. Others may encounter the exact same information and then label, store, and retrieve it in completely different ways.

When you insist on your own perceptions and conclusions as *the* truth, you run the risk of alienating others and severely limiting possible solution sets. The opportunity here is to review your old files, rigorously examine them for current applicability, and then open them for new, incoming information. As you do so, you will begin to see that those around you may be perceiving things differently and arriving at differing recommendations about what can be done. To lead powerfully and build an effective team, base your leadership on the mosaic created through collection and sharing of realities.

> *A Self-Management Practice*
>
> Try flexing your muscle memory by using one of the skills you picked up in a previous chapter: the one about using "I" statements. When you are exploring truths with others, you are basically sharing Filing Cabinets to uncover the most helpful perspectives or, better yet, provoke conversations that none of you would have foreseen on your own. When you say, "Here's my reality" or "Here's my take on it" when sharing your perspective, you are participating in a productive way. You are signaling that this is your own truth; you are not intending to have the only answer.

An example of differing realities occurs when you walk by a new construction site with a high fence around it. Curiosity takes hold and you find a hole to peer through. You have your view and quickly form your idea of what is being built behind the barrier. Your friend who was walking down the other street did the same thing, except he was looking through a different hole from another direction and has an entirely different view. As you two ask around, you find seven others who have yet different interpretations. When you get together to talk about it, which do you think will be more productive—to dig in and demand that your *truth* is adopted by the whole group, to vote on which individual's perspective is right, or to all put your heads together, compare notes, and create a composite reality? How many times have you dug in with your *truth* in discussions with work associates or family members?

Opening up to other viewpoints gives you the ability to combine other "truths" with yours to produce new ideas and richer approaches. This is a time to listen newly, be present, and take yourself lightly! Discern new possibilities from other's perspectives and reach more productive levels of dialogue and interaction. Declaring that there is nothing wrong or broken will displace the brain space that opinions and judgments usually occupy and open higher-level pathways of thinking that are usually narrowed by those opinions and judgments. Committing to uncovering shared reality in the present moment will greatly increase your ability to let go of your attachment to the past records in your File Cabinet and generously support others in stepping beyond theirs. Remember that your truths are just a subset of all possible truths!

My Ideas are a Subset of All Ideas

Exploring Other's "truths"

> *Declare that each person's contributions are valid and valuable.*

Unrelenting change brings up new and often complex issues requiring new solutions. The ability to draw out and stimulate creativity, agility, and collaboration from as many people as possible and turn new ideas into productive action in fulfilling the Yonder Star is essential. Free and open exchanges, quick shifts in thinking and action, and reorganizing in a new way required to deliver the new ideas becomes a regular mandate. To be successful in this reality, it is essential to have maximum involvement in fluid and open conversations. Often the best ideas are sparked by what another person says and developed by building on the comments of others. Declaring that each person's contribution is valid and valuable is a declaration that creates a supportive context for such discussions.

We are not saying that the declaration that each person's contributions are valid and valuable is a declaration that works every time or is even appropriate in all situations. The coach of a professional hockey team who declares each player's contributions valid and valuable may be making a very humane declaration, and it is one that could find the coach seeking a career in some other industry in short order. The same might be true for your attorney in a trial.

This declaration is, however, crucial to creating an environment of mutual trust, respect, and safety, and is a prerequisite to exploring truths with others. You won't even get to hear much in the way of another person's perspective without it. You will learn more about the importance of creating a safe, productive environment later when we discuss Operating Principle #8, *Make it Safe and Productive*.

This exploration of *truths* with others is an important part of group process to separate and distinguish opinions from "ground truth" observable data. By listening and sorting through conclusions, interpretations, and inferences to identify mutually observable and verifiable facts and data, you and your team will be able to create agreement on a starting point based on data that everyone is seeing in the same light. One of the simplest examples of this point is the situation already described where people view a construction site from many different angles. Arguing from each participant's conclusions about what is being built will not be as effective as sharing observable data that can then be analyzed in its composite form. By combining forces and getting to a place where individual observations produce a broader shared reality, the group has positioned itself powerfully to generate creative solutions.

Asking questions opens the door to the unknown. You have to be willing to receive an answer you don't agree with or don't want to hear. It takes courage to ask questions.

Tom Batchelder–*Barking Up a Dead Horse*

Get Really Good at Asking Exploring Questions

To be able to effectively "explore truths," it pays to get really good at asking questions—questions that help illuminate rather than criticize or depose. When clients first begin to practice asking questions, one of their major pitfalls is to disguise answers in their questions or to "lead the witness." Learn to ask open ended questions of yourself and others. For a list of sample questions, see the Practical Application— Section Five of this book for *Questions to Explore Reality—Curiosity versus Interrogation.*

Why Is Exploring "truths" Important?

You cannot be a valuable contributor in a dialogue while pushing your version of reality as truth. When you show willingness to consider your own truth as one viewpoint and own it as such using "I" statements, you open up conversational possibilities rather than shut them down. Your group, team, or family is missing a huge opportunity for increased collaboration and effectiveness unless you all learn to have discussions that honor and appreciate varied, even conflicting viewpoints, and learn to sort opinions, assessments, and labels from what actually happened. What is the ground truth? Inquire, ask, be curious, then inquire some more. Collaboration becomes more fluid and a more powerful and effective way to work than interacting based on past experiences of going it alone or in disagreement with others.

The result of *not* being open to and investigating all the perspectives in a situation can be dramatic. If some participants do not experience that their commitments, circumstances, and points of view matter, you may unwittingly set up a situation where important information is withheld and participation is suppressed. Any decisions ignoring these unexamined perspectives could lead you down a path of failed actions. Each person may walk away from a discussion still tightly holding on to his or her own ideas. Worse yet, participants may agree to disagree, which does nothing to increase conversational capacities or forward fulfillment of the Yonder Star.

> *Agreeing to disagree is a way of giving up—an admission that neither one of us has the skills, courage, or tenacity to work it out!*

What Difference Does it Make?

My Solution Set Grows!

When all participants feel they're being heard and appreciated for what they hold as their truths, they are more prone to open up, collaborate, and envision more creative solutions together. As you and others examine various perspectives (truths) together, you begin to realize that you are beginning to describe a whole that encompasses the differing perspectives and may even be a much richer and more powerful view than any individual had at the start.

In addition, when you show that you are willing to examine your own truths and are interested in others, you are demonstrating an important quality of leadership. You are setting up an environment where capitalizing and expanding on each other's ideas, flexing new conversational capacities, and growing into a cohesive, positive, problem-solving group comes easily, even when the toughest issues must be addressed and resolved.

When Exploring truths Is Missing:

- A lot of monologues take place, the one with the loudest voice or most power "wins," and others appease.

- Only past based solutions with historical evidence get considered.

- You slip into convince-and-convert language, dueling File Cabinets dominate, and struggles for domination get characterized as "healthy, passionate discussions."

- Valuable input and perspectives get shut down or wasted, and you and others carry away the same ideas you started with—no new learning occurs.

- Little or no progress is made toward the Yonder Star.

When This Principle Is in Play:

- You approach a conversation ready to review and reconsider your own perspective.

- You ask curious, open-ended questions to explore other's perspectives.

- You use "I" statements when sharing your own views and experience.

- Productive sharing of File Cabinet experiences takes place.

- New ideas and solutions emerge that were not available prior to your discussion.

- There has been a shift from "I agree/disagree" to "That is a different perspective, tell me more."

- Differences occur to you as a trigger for your curiosity mind-set and further exploration.

Case Study: Explore *truths:* Mine, Theirs and Ours

The Cost of Rigidity

Matt's new Marketing VP shared his pride in being a U.S. manufacturer and proposed an advertising campaign around the theme of "Made in America." Matt asked him to present the plan at the next Executive team meeting to gather constructive feedback.

A key assumption in the VP's presentation was "American consumers will pay more for American-made products." Several executives asked for more clarification asking, "Is there a new study out?" While a bit impatient at the interruption to his presentation's flow, he answered, "No there is not a study that I know of, but here's how we know it is true:

- We sell more in our booths at trade shows than the booths that sell imports.
- Our distributors tell us they sell more of our products than the imports.
- Customers placing orders say they prefer our products over the imports because our products take less time and cost less to install and we've got really tricky designs."

His recommendation was shaped (and limited) by his belief and pride that "Made in America" was right and best. As the group asked additional clarifying questions, the VP became very defensive. For him, his perception was *the truth*, and anyone who challenged that truth was attacking him *and* attacking patriotism.

The recommendations from the group were to re-examine that premise and get some good third-party customer research. In the end, Matt did not approve the plan. The VP's unwillingness to openly and willingly explore his truths on this subject turned out to be a recurring theme. Eventually, his attachment to his positions cost him his job.

Case Study: Explore *truths:* Mine, Theirs and Ours

New File Cabinet—New Relationship

One of our clients has a great dad-daughter story he tells this way:

"We were going through what I think is fairly typical sixteen-year-old stuff, and my wife and I were having these conversations about Susan—that 'her room's a mess, she's so disorganized, her life's always a drama, and when things go wrong, she blames everyone else, mostly us, for everything that's wrong in her life. She's selfish, emotional, and irrational.' That's how our File Cabinet was for Susan. With those listening filters, what do you think we got from her? Disorganized, selfish…all the evidence to support our opinions!

"After having spent time in a 2130 Partners session on our mental File Cabinets, I went home, sat down with my wife, and asked, 'Can we examine the contents of our Filing Cabinet and our listening filters for Susan?' She agreed and we listed our complaints (filters) that we'd been listening through and interacting from and the frustration and all the drama that was there.

"I then asked, 'Is there another set of evidence out there?' We noted that she is a 4.0 GPA student and is getting a tennis scholarship. She has good friends that think the world of her. She's smart and she's funny. All of those statements were equally true.

"We made a conscious decision to start listening to Susan through a new filter of an incredible young woman who was going to make a great contribution to the world if we could get out of the way and just love her. Our relationship with Susan quickly changed.

"I just got an e-mail from her from college, where she is now a junior. It said, 'Hey, Dad, I was having a conversation with my roommate and I realized that I missed your expertise and advice. There is stuff that's been on my mind and hasn't necessarily been expressed.' Then she described her troubles with a boyfriend and love and commitment and all that stuff. She ended with, 'I don't know where I'm going with this, but I figured that I would send it your way. I love you very much and I'm really glad I can turn to you for advice. I cannot imagine my life without you and I believe that I'm lucky to have you as a role model always. Get back to me when you have a chance. I love you very, very much. Susan.'

"So this is how she's relating to me now, five years later. I realize that my new listening for her as a great human being created a possibility for a very different relationship than one that might have come from my past critical File Cabinet listening. This isn't the only benefit I've gotten from exploring my own truths in my File Cabinet since that session. I have to say, though, if it were the only result, it was well worth it!"

Practice Opportunities:
Explore *truths*: Mine, Theirs, and Ours

Create a Breakthrough

Do you want to create a real breakthrough in your organization or family? Take on one of those difficult "don't want to deal with it" issues that have been hanging around in your life or business, investigate the "realities" of it, yours and theirs, and wrestle it to a solution. Make what you thought was an unattainable goal become a situation where everyone feels good about having the courage to confront the issue and bring it to a resolution that works for all. That means being willing to have as many conversations as necessary to make that happen. New conversational capacities will be built *and* relationships will be enhanced!

Get Really Good at Asking Exploring Questions

To strengthen your exploration muscle, pick a few situations, both personal and professional, and craft a list of questions that would help explore reality and illuminate the situation and perspectives. Be sure your questions are 'other-centered" meaning that they are intended to help the other person illuminate something for themselves rather that gathering data for yourself. For a list of sample questions, see the Practical Application—Section Five of this book for *Questions to Explore Reality—Curiosity versus Interrogation*. Then get present, engage, have a new conversation, listen newly to their responses! Stay at it and be willing to let go of repeated failures. It's natural and part of the process.

Operating Principle #6:

Confront and Deal with Real Issues

The most challenging aspect of this operating principle is learning to reframe what you think "confronting" means and what real issues are.

Confront Issues and Challenges—Not Each Other

Many times in our workshops, we get resistance to using the word "confront." It seems to call up mental pictures of dominating behavior, red faces, protruding neck veins, or someone standing in another's face, yelling. Clearly, this is not a condition that is even remotely consistent with productive interactions. Shift that focus to one of confronting *the issue,* together with another person, not confronting the other person.

To be effective, subscribe to a different definition and connotation of the word, one that goes to the basic construction of the word "confront." *Con* in many languages means "with" or "together"—as in chili con carne (chili with meat), or the words condolence (to grieve with), concur (to run together), confab (to chat together), or configure (to shape together). So if you view the word by its etymology from Latin, it means, "to be with, in front of." This brings in the notion of teamwork, to be together regarding something, to stand in front of something (the issue) together. Stand together in a learning mode in confronting and dealing with your shared situation. Focus on the issue itself, distinct from the people and personalities involved.

A more traditional conversation, confronting a person (in this case an example of a direct report) rather than the real issue, might be, "Tom, you are supposed to have this project done by Thursday. You haven't done anything. You'd better get your tail in gear. You have no room for screwing it up (again?)!" Shifting to confronting the issue (using "I" statements) with the other person, your conversation might be, "Tom, this project is scheduled to be completed by Thursday and I've not seen any progress since our last meeting. What is in the way or what is missing to have it be completed on time?"

Great Solution, Now What is the Issue You Actually Want to Sort Out and Solve?

The second essential aspect of living this Operating Principle is to learn to recognize and explore for the real, underlying issues. We use the metaphors of **roadblocks** and **potholes** to represent the real issues and challenges to identify in order to determine the most highly leveraged actions available. Roadblocks are real or perceived barriers in your pathway to fulfilling your Yonder Star. Can you remove the obstacle or barrier or must you find a new path around it? Potholes are things that are missing that would get you into action in a highly productive way. With regard to potholes, ask, "What's missing that, if we filled it in, would pave the way to our Yonder Star?" One of the biggest challenges in becoming highly productive, whether individually or as a team, is to be able to sort these real barriers and "missings" from all of the possible issues and activities in front of you and to focus on addressing them in a collaborative way.

Real Issues: What is in the way of our Yonder Star?

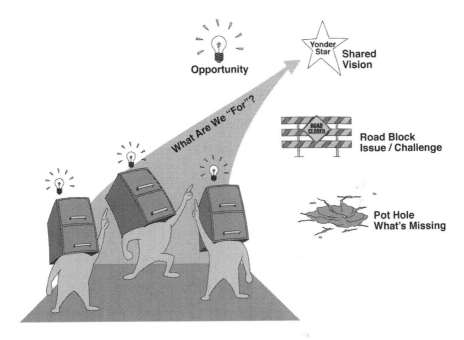

To explore for the real issues, it sometimes takes getting at the issues underneath the first ones thrown on the table. The real issues that everyone is uncomfortable talking about or has given up pursuing because resolution has always been avoided are often masked by these superficial topics. Sometimes, these issues can be several years old and hanging around because no one is willing to take them on. There is no reason to proceed any further unless and until the "elephant in the room" is acknowledged.

A difficulty you almost certainly will encounter in exploring for real issues is the hidden wall that you or others have built around certain topics—"the undiscussables." What is it that is going unsaid and unaddressed? The proverbial "elephant in the room" that no one is willing to talk about during a meeting sets up a status quo and relegates the important conversations to a gossipy discussion in the restroom at the break. The meaningful discussion that, if tackled, would really move the team forward will continue to drift. Then the balance of the discussion will be built over the top of the unresolved issue, and no real breakthroughs will occur.

Create an Environment Where Real Issues Can Surface

The key to being able to tackle these real issues and achieve high levels of group effectiveness lies in creating and maintaining an atmosphere of mutual trust, respect, and safety. In that atmosphere participants can and will raise the "unmentionables" without fear of censorship or other unwanted consequences.

The first important step in the process is to do a quick audit to assure that you are collectively working from the frame of reference offered by the Operating Principles discussed so far. Does it feel safe to bring up the really crucial and maybe unpopular aspects of the issue? Is everyone participating openly and freely? Ask yourself and the group, are you all:

- Present and focused on *this* issue or topic?

- Releasing your white-knuckled grip on your own opinion, defensiveness or righteous solution?

- Listening appreciatively and openly to other perspectives?

- Trading judgment for curiosity?

Set up a productive environment by being present, listening newly, exploring truths, and declaring nothing is wrong or broken. Next, move your focus out and up by asking, "What is the bigger goal that this issue is tied to?" or "What is our Yonder Star?" It could be as big-picture and strategic as the overall long-term vision or as immediate as "What is it we really intend to make happen in this meeting?" Now you are ready to address real issues together.

Being clear about the essential nature of a productive environment is especially important to your ability to confront and deal with real issues. All interactions are more effective when participants experience that they share mutual trust, respect, and safety, and are connected with the others in the discussion. When you feel that you are valued for your input, you can rely upon others to be supportive, even while having your viewpoint questioned, and you can speak without fear of ridicule or retribution. When this condition is present, it is far easier to open up to possibility and the potential in the issue at hand.

> If you set out to really deal with a tough issue, the environment around you must be free of threats, domination, and disrespect, or the discussion will be cut short, everyone will duck for cover, and you will be back to square one. We will dig more deeply into this topic in the next section on Productive Dialogues.

Real Issues Can Be Masked by Misdiagnosis

> A *problem named is a problem half solved* is an applicable quote attributed to a number of sources with various phrasing.
>
> Dwight has a correlate to this quote: *A problem misnamed is a problem stuck.*

In most effective groups, the real issue that has things stuck is a different issue (the "real issue") than the one presented at the start of the conversation. If it weren't, the individual or group that is stuck would have, in most cases, already solved the issue and gone on about the next tasks. The Operating Principle *Listen Newly, Be Intentionally Slow to Understand* works well to help you listen just a bit longer than "jumping to conclusions," which often causes superficial misdiagnoses. Patience and good, open-ended questions that help the participants uncover the real issue are key to discovering what is really keeping things stuck. Without conscious attention to this idea, many people spend their energy asking questions that satisfy their own curiosity rather than those that expand the listener's thinking and perspective. Some people cleverly disguise their solutions and "shoulds" as a question! When we are facilitating issue resolution conversations, we often spend a good deal of time having the group ask "clarifying questions only" with the emphasis on clarification for the person bringing the issue to the table.

When the real underlying issue is identified, problem solving usually flows quickly and easily. On balance, the majority of the available time is best spent exploring for real, underlying issues and a much smaller portion of the time creating answers.

Use the Three Levels of Conversational Impact as a Diagnostic

If you are in the middle of a conversation with someone and the discussion turns heated, sullen, or just plain stuck, stop speaking! *It is impossible to successfully forward your agenda in the face of an upset—whether it is yours or the other person's.* You've reached a place where the focus has shifted from confronting the issue together to focusing on each other, on being right, bulldozing agendas, proving the other person wrong, or protecting yourself. As a result, the topic itself gets stalled and your relationship can even take a hit.

Three Levels of Conversational Impact

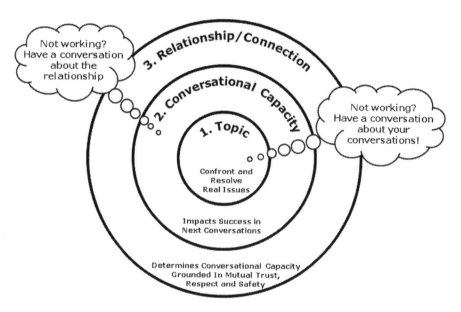

Take a deep breath, ask to reschedule, or in some way take a time out. Before starting in on the controversial topic again, have a conversation about your conversation. In addition to having an unresolved topic, you also now have an unproductive conversation as an issue to resolve. Don't miss this cue. There is a Practical Application to help you format this kind of conversation: *Have a Conversation About Your Conversations: Building Conversational Capacities.*

Essentially, a conversation about your conversations focuses on how to design a more productive interaction about that topic, and about all of your tough topics. Acknowledge your part in the last one and suggest what you could do differently in the next conversation about the topic or issue. Ask the other person what they see as a productive framework to set up a successful interaction about a volatile topic. Being able to talk about the things that trigger each of you or get in the way of working productively together will not necessarily have them go away. By bringing them to conscious discussion, they will lose their grip on you and are less likely to derail the conversation when they arise in the future.

These types of conversations build conversational capacities— your collaborative muscles. It may initially seem that this kind of conversation takes the focus away from the *real* issue and takes time away from the important work at hand. At this point, however, the most immediate issue is that the two of you can't have a productive conversation about that topic, and maybe not about any topic! By recognizing this, you can stop, recover, and then redirect your focus to rebuilding the relationship through exploring your shared truths and focusing on mutually observable data.

If you are both upset, which seems most often to be the case, clear yourself first. Notice that you are upset, breathe out, and get yourself back present. Next ask the other person, "What happened?" and let the person share so that he or she can get back to being present as well. This puts both of you on much more solid ground so that you can return to working on the issue again with better results. If you are not getting to a reset point, you may have to reschedule. Start the next meeting with connecting and setting the Yonder Star for the discussion. Check the Practical Application: *From Upset to Productivity—Uncovering and Speaking Commitment.*

Why Is Confronting and Dealing with the Real Issue Important?

If you and others are in a relationship built on mutual trust, respect, and safety, you can talk about pretty much any issue and get it resolved as partners or as a team. By dealing head-on with underlying issues as a team that is committed to fulfilling a Yonder Star, you are taking a giant step toward eliminating the waste and friction in your interactions, building your conversational capacities, and contributing to a stronger working relationship. Conversations that used to involve dancing around or avoiding difficult or untouchable subjects become much less distracting and time consuming. Conversations based solely on proving who is right are replaced by mutual sharing of ideas and experience aimed at resolution and based on movement toward a shared Yonder Star.

When you start from a place where you are focusing on discovering and addressing real, underlying issues instead of initial, superficial, conclusions or interpretations, you can base the discussion on your shared truths and bring energy to bear in the creative dimension. Resources are not wasted on chasing mistaken or unimportant issues when everyone is freed up to hone in on the core.

What Difference Does It Make?

Instead of spending lots of time rehashing old issues or working around them, you confront and resolve real issues and accelerate your progress on fulfilling your Yonder Star. A group that learns how to identify what's underlying the current situation and willingly deals with it has high productivity and high organizational value. You can create a lean team that can work through a difficult situation, putting it to rest without hesitation or delay.

When 'Confront and Deal with Real Issues' is Missing:

- You find it's easier to continue to discuss what has been broken in the past than it is to address current issues, so a lot of time is spent wasted in hindsight.

- Everyone is carefully stepping around the main challenges, looking to solve hypothetical situations rather than face the difficult real ones right in front of them.

- Great ideas and solutions are generated only at the surface level, leaving underlying issues untouched.

- Conversations break down over personal issues or people confronting each other rather than the issues.

- Your focus has shifted from the Yonder Star to someone or something else.

When This Principle Is in Play:

- Your focus is on the gap—you can identify and prioritize the "what's missing" between your current circumstances and your Yonder Star.

- You are skilled at defining the issue and separating it from the person or people involved.

- You and all the others commit to doing the heavy lifting by raising and confronting issues that no one wanted to touch, clearing the path to the Yonder Star.

- You create and nurture an environment of mutual trust, respect, and safety.

- You use "and" rather than "but" to bring attention to the coexistence of multiple perspectives. (For a deeper discussion and examples of replacing "but" with "and," see the Practical Applications—Section Five: *Eliminate the Buts*.)

Case Study: Confront and Deal with the Real Issues

Scarcity—The Real Issue

We had worked on a number of topics with Dennis, the third-generation entrepreneurial leader of his family's manufacturing and retail firm, including sales strategy, personnel, manufacturing and distribution, customer service and intergenerational ownership and yet the firm just never seemed to grow or make much money. One day, as we were working yet another seemingly typical issue with Dennis, a new insight popped up: "Dennis, here is what is underlying all of our discussions. You and your family have been running your firm in a scarcity mentality! For years, the mindset has been "not enough" in almost every case; not enough money, not enough time, not enough good people, not enough customers." With a frame of reference or set of filters based on scarcity (which was invisible to them all), Dennis and his team only gathered data that verified that worldview. Any actions taken were also shaped by this unrecognized belief and therefore always produced results that verified their view.

Dennis, who had been a bit glazed over during the discussion, froze for a few long seconds, sat bolt upright, began to grin, and exclaimed, "Unbelievable! You are so right!" Once the real issue was unearthed, he knew what to do. He shifted his perspective, his speaking, his questions, and the framework of his leadership from scarcity to "What's missing to close the gap between our Yonder Star and our current level of results?" Dennis soon had the firm growing rapidly to a sustained 20 percent year-over-year same-store sales growth with excellent profitability.

Case Study: Confront and Deal with the Real Issues

From Delusion to Action

Terry had been wrestling for some time with what to do with his "irresponsible" son, who showed little interest in any fatherly advice. Don was in his twenties, living at home, not working, in a huge amount of debt, and seemingly not committed to anything except hanging around the house or with his girlfriend (when they weren't arguing). Don would often pit mom against dad to get what he wanted, while continuing in his self-justifying world, pretending he was doing just fine. After an extended and fruitless effort to enroll his wife in kicking Don out of the house, Terry asked if Don would work with one of our coaches. Amazingly, Don agreed and they got to work.

Don's coach is a master at "ruthless compassion" and works very quickly. She pushed him to take off his blinders. Within a few short months, they had raised and discussed the real underlying issues. Don had taken a hard look at each area of his life and relationships and his excuses for each condition. He dug in and started looking for a job, began to confront real issues with his girlfriend, and started thinking about a direction for his life. With his coach's support, he grew his ability to self-reflect and self-intervene, the basis of Self-Generated Accountability.

As he gained strength, he launched a series of aggressive lifestyle initiatives. He ended his relationship with his girlfriend, moved to another state, stopped smoking, started back to school, got a job, and created his own Yonder Star for his life. Confronting and dealing with a series of real issues, instead of continuing to pretend they didn't exist, gave Don a new lease on life, and the energy to be in action. Since Don's parent's *real* Yonder Star for Don was to see him as a happy, productive, self-supporting, contributing citizen, they were both thrilled.

Practice Opportunities:
Confront and Deal with the Real Issues

Will the Real Issues Please Stand Up?

Use your own situations to identity which of the issue-masking conditions could be applicable.

Five Issue-Masking Pitfalls:

1. Accepting a surface or generalized description or label
2. Misdiagnosis
3. Avoiding
4. Blaming and making it personal
5. Hiding or masking in humor

Uncovering the real issues requires skill at asking the right questions of yourself and others. Practice developing yourself in the art of asking clarifying questions that are designed to get to the real issues and to open up the mental framework in which you and others have been thinking about the issue. That means asking open-ended questions when working with others rather than those for which a "yes" or "no" or data might end the exchange.
   Ask yourself these questions:

- Am I falling for the first or seemingly expeditious diagnosis and sacrificing the opportunity to identify and resolve the underlying issue?
- Is there a pitfall that seems to be a recurring theme for me?
- Am I confronting a person rather than the issue?
- Am I disguising my solutions as questions?
- Who else could be helpful to me in further identifying the real issues?

Section Four:

Now Get Engaged

Productive Dialogue

Build your reputation as "a leader around whom issues get raised and resolved productively"

The Essential Notions and Operating Principles comprise the interventions into and additions to your past mental operating system that enable you to build the capacity to model and foster engagement and collaboration with those around you. These upgrades give you the opening to have authentic conversations and relationships and be more creative in your thinking about virtually every business and personal situation you encounter. After reading and working through the Essential Notions, you studied and applied the Operating Principles listed in Section Two "It Begins With Me–Self-Generated Accountability." There you learned the value of the leadership practices of being present, listening newly and taking yourself lightly.

In the last section, you added in three more Operating Principles that are important to productive collaboration. These Operating Principles allow a broader view of reality, help prevent defensiveness and survival brain thinking, and encourage conversations that deal with the goal, the current condition, and the gap between them. You learned to "explore truths" and confront and deal with real issues, all with a curious, problem solving mind-set. In this section we offer three more Operating Principles that when combined with the others, support the ultimate objective of Productive Dialogue.

The purpose of dialogue is to create something new–something that has not been thought previously by any participant prior to the dialogue.

Investing your thought processes to establish a Productive Dialogue takes courage and commitment. This is the defining activity you have been building toward as you have been working with the material in this book. Productive Dialogue will be the basis for effectively addressing and moving beyond roadblocks and potholes that you encounter in the process of fulfilling your Yonder Star.

> **Dialogue:** from the Greek roots *dia* ("through") and *logos* ("meaning"); therefore, a productive dialogue is one in which meaning flows through.

Said simply, a Productive Dialogue is an interaction between two or more people where issues are raised and resolved productively or new, previously unthought-of innovations are created. The parties' respective intentions and perspectives are clearly shared and issues—the roadblocks and potholes to progress—are confronted in a direct and open way. This process involves openly and collaboratively exploring the choices available or created through the interaction rather than simply two or more monologues running simultaneously. It usually leads to a course of action that is both more productive and more satisfying to the participants. Often it produces real breakthroughs where historical barriers may have existed at the start of the conversation. When it is done well, everyone's File Cabinets are opened and free, and fluid sharing takes place that stimulates high levels of creativity and unforeseen outcomes.

As you encounter the roadblocks and potholes you will be able to:

- recreate the alignment you achieved at the start of a project or campaign;

- make new, fresh choices as to the best actions to take;

- get into action more quickly than ever.

In a productive dialogue, participants willingly share their File Cabinet contents—perspectives, experiences, and knowledge—with an intention to contribute. An elegant, robust solution is more important, and fulfilling the shared Yonder Star is more important, than credit.

Productive Dialogue Zone

The Productive Dialogue Zone diagram first presented in the Essential Notions—Section One is repeated here to remind you of where to place your focus—what you are aiming toward. It requires both a relationship *and* a results focus.

The Productive Dialogue Zone

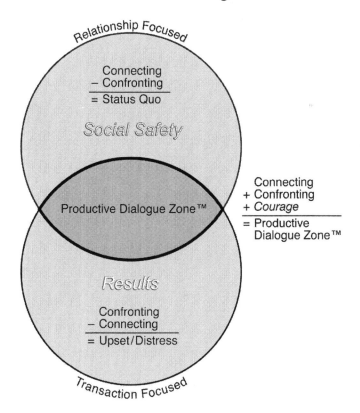

In the Productive Dialogue Zone you are connected to the other person, aware of their view of the world, and together you are confronting the issue or challenge in the gap between current conditions and your shared Yonder Star. It takes courage combined with connecting and confronting to be successfully operating in the Productive Dialogue Zone. It takes courage to enter into a tough conversation with another person, be present and intentional, and not know beforehand how you are going to exit the conversation! It takes even more conscious intention and courage to stay present and engaged in the conversation if it gets rough or you begin to have thoughts like "we're never going to get through this" or "I have absolutely no idea what to say now!"

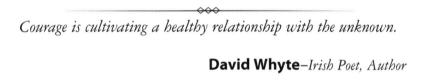

Courage is cultivating a healthy relationship with the unknown.

David Whyte–*Irish Poet, Author*

You have to work your way through it, moment by moment. When *you* have developed your ability to work effectively in the Productive Dialogue Zone, you will have a high level of *collaborative capacities*, an essential leadership attribute. When *your team* has developed themselves to work effectively in the Productive Dialogue Zone, they have created a high level of *collaborative capital*. A team (or family) that regularly generates creative, innovative, and effective solutions has greater collaborative capital than merely the sum of collective capacities of all of the individuals.

We have not yet met any individual or team (or family) who manages to stay in the Productive Dialogue Zone 100% of the time with 100% of the issues. Some issues tend to knock you off your center more than others. The key to mastering the Productive Dialogue Zone is to self-correct.

- Notice when it's not working and bring yourself back present to the current condition.

- Ask "What happened?" "What threw us off track?"

- Reconnect to your Yonder Star and the shared Yonder Star.

- Get curious, ask questions—get back in the game. The only time you are really defeated is if you give up or let fear defeat you.

Years ago, in a workshop with Sheila Heen and Doug Stone, authors of *Difficult Conversations: How to Discuss What Matters Most*, Sheila explained to our group: "We called them difficult conversations because they are difficult!"

In this section, with the additional operating principles, your mindset and skills at interacting with others to fulfill your shared Yonder Star will become focused and refined, and you will have begun to truly upgrade your mental operating system. Learn the leadership practices to create an environment for powerful, collaborative interaction even in the face of fear, resistance, and unrelenting change. Take the time to respect and fully integrate these dimensions and be engaged—you'll be amazed at the results. Practice in real life situations as you read along in the book. It will make your learning more real and much more durable. There are several examples of specific types of conversations in the Practical Applications—Section Five. Be sure to check out: *Productive Delegation—Building Confidence and Accountability* and *Dialogue for Making a Role Change or Closing a Performance Gap*.

Operating Principle #7:

Be Responsible for Creating Value

Freedom lies in the ability to be responsible for my experiences.

The highest state of practice with regard to being responsible for creating value is to hold yourself accountable at some level for everything you are experiencing in your interactions. We are not saying that this is the truth. We are pointing out that if you engage with life this way, you will see new ways of interacting and new conversations you can have that will lead you much closer to your ideal and your Yonder Star.

There is an important difference in the quality of your experiences and the resulting outcomes when you take on responsibility for creating value in your own experiences rather than looking for value from your circumstances and from others.

In fact, we have observed in our groups over the years that around year two or three, a member will either leave or step up to a new level of owning their experience and participation. They are either done grazing and getting all the goodies they have judged valuable, or they realize that the real goodies are in being a contribution to others and generating value for themselves.

The group members that successfully continue in the groups for many years discover that their own willingness and contribution to value creation is what makes the difference in their experience and in the experience of others. They don't sit back during a group discussion or make a guest speaker wrong when they are not initially experiencing value. They engage, ask questions, say what's missing for them (using "I" statements), or add something to the conversation that moves it to a new level.

In fact, the highest-level performers have actually learned that there can't be any value from the experience until they are coming from, or have a mind-set of, value creation themselves. Operating from this mind-set shifts your perceptions regarding what the other person has to say. Their contributions take on whole new meaning and the other person is stimulated to offer up even more value.

It's in Your Thinking, Speaking, and Your Listening

It's your mind-set. It's your choice. Who else can really be responsible for your attitude and approach? It takes drawing on most of the previous Operating Principles presented in this book to consciously create value for yourself and others. The trigger point for loss of your value-creating capacities is when your mind slips to judgment, right/wrong, boredom, or impatience. Presence, taking yourself lightly, and displacing your own truths are all required to be able to generate a valuable way of listening.

Listening from this principle allows you to hear things differently, which will open up new pathways for learning and collaboration. Mickey Connolly and Richard Rianoshek, PhD, of Conversant Solutions, LLC, call it "generative listening" versus "consumptive listening." You are either in "do it to me mode" or you are actively engaged, either laying back or leaning in. Practicing this principle includes your ability to listen newly and be intentionally slow to understand. As the listener you create a receptacle for value so value can show up.

When you speak from this principle, it means you are building on comments and ideas of others and are drawing out the value in the conversation. You are asking clarifying questions to more fully understand the topic or the other person's perspective. You speak up when you don't understand something or have been distracted by your attachment to contents of your own File Cabinet.

A Self-Management Practice

Picture yourself just before going into a meeting to discuss a problem that has come up time and time again because "people aren't willing to change the way they operate." You notice yourself groaning and complaining, thinking how awful the next hour is going to be. What outcome do you think will be produced with that mind-set?

Alternatively, you can take on creating value for yourself and others at the meeting. Commit to leaving the meeting with a feeling of accomplishment. Notice that you are at the Leadership Choice Point, where you can choose to be either a victim or "The Boss of Me." What attitude and behavior might you choose as you enter the room? What Yonder Star might you create for your participation? For the meeting? For the group? Are you willing to take on enrolling your fellow group members in the Yonder Star of a valuable and productive meeting for everyone?

As you move through all the ups and downs in the conversation, you'll get a second read on whether you really had a powerful intention at the start. If you are experiencing value, you did. If not, you were kidding yourself. Practice self-observation and learn to distinguish an authentic intention from a good idea, a "wouldn't it be nice if," or a "should."

Author W. Somerset Maugham said: "It's a funny thing about life; if you refuse to accept anything but the best, you very often get it." If the best for you is great value both for yourself and others and you engage in interactions with that clear intention, you really will experience outcomes that could not have been predicted otherwise.

You are the Source of Value!

It is important to remember that no one else can create value for you unless you are first willing to bring an intention for value to the encounter.

It starts with a clear intention to create value for yourself and others while you are in the conversation or meeting by engaging in productive dialogue with the others toward that end. The effectiveness of any conversations you launch will be a direct function of your intention and the level of collaborative capacities you have built by invoking the Operating Principles through your ongoing practice.

Absent intention, the rest will be gesture. In the absence of intention your past-based File Cabinet fueled reactions are all that you have available. With intention, you can practice curiosity listening—listening carefully and being slow to understand other participants' contributions to the topic. You can ask open-ended questions that provoke further exploration and discussion.

Your path may not run smoothly, especially when you first start to work with your new collaborative capacities. Just as most of the prior Operating Principles can support you in practicing this one, the absence of the previous Operating Principles will reduce your capacity for value creation.

You may find yourself falling back as your mind rushes to argument or one-upmanship, or wanders to thoughts of your upcoming vacation. Just catch yourself and return yourself to the present. Embark on the Yonder Star line in the Leadership Choice Point model again by choosing to create value for yourself and for others. Keep noticing as your mind drifts off to other work or personal issues or is distracted by your phone messages or PDA. It is normal and practically unavoidable.

Choose curiosity, being present in the moment again, and engage. Ask questions that explore current reality as you and others perceive it, so you can begin to create a collage of ideas that lead to real problem solving and fulfillment of the immediate Yonder Star. Check in regularly to see how you are doing on creating value for yourself and others.

> When Dwight first started working with his Vistage groups, he was surprised to note that one of the regular practices several members had was what he called "voting on the speaker" and engaging in mild campaigns to enroll others in their view. Once or twice they had successfully demoralized the speaker by the first break! The practice didn't make sense and seemed to him to diminish or destroy any ability to get or add value to the experience.
>
> As a speaker, Suzanne has experienced this for herself. After one session she remembers having the facilitator announce, "OK, we always critique the speaker afterwards, so are you ready?" That is a certain set-up for judgmental listening—a far cry from constructive feedback or listening and participating for value. An accompanying practice is what we call "television listening"—"OK, I am comfortable, now entertain me!"
>
> Once the members had loaded up the Operating Principles, essentially all of those old behaviors disappeared. Members now engage with a speaker, challenge the discussion, and are very involved. Afterwards they most often talk about their high level of takeaway and what a good job the speaker did. In some cases the speaker ends up delivering a different experience than even they were expecting and will often comment about what a great group it is. No surprise. How often do you engage this way in each and every meeting or interaction?

Why Is Being Responsible for Creating Value Important?

We started this final Operating Principles section by discussing Productive Dialogue. Your intention to interact in a manner that creates value determines how productive a dialogue can be. This Operating Principle is an intervention into your instant, automatic, historical mind-set. If you approach a meeting or encounter with the intention of contributing and receiving value, you set up an environment where participants feel safe, respected, and comfortable in participating and the Learning Zone can be expanded for the participants in the group. In addition, such an intention makes you more receptive to new ideas and opinions, stretching and flexing your capacities in being present, listening, understanding others' perspectives, and discovering shared reality.

What Difference Does It Make?

You will achieve much higher levels of satisfaction in your relationships. For you personally, taking on the mind-set that you can and will generate value will give you a tremendous shift in your learning capacities. You will be more present, engaged, curious, attentive, and, at a minimum, certainly not bored. As you practice, new collaborative capacities get developed that are transferable to many other situations. This way of being becomes more automatic for you than the automatic File Cabinet critic.

Since others see you engaged in the process and really listening, they start speaking up, feeling that their contributions will be heard. They appreciate your practice of producing value in the situation and get inspired to join in working toward a common goal. It is unlikely that people will walk away saying, "Well, that was a worthless meeting…" or "I never should have started a conversation with her!"

When Being Responsible for Creating Value Is Missing:

- You are bored, impatient, or disengaged, or sit back and expect to be entertained.

- Your automatic File Cabinet critic is busy counting the number of "ums" or "ahs."

- You have decided it is your job to judge and determine whose contribution is really valuable and valid before you listen.

- You aren't present or taking yourself (or your preconceived notions) lightly.

- You contribute to an *unproductive* environment, diminishing mutual trust, respect or safety.

- You leave the encounter with all your preconceptions and prejudices safely in place.

When This Principle Is in Play:

- You approach the meeting or conversation with the intention to get the most out of the interaction and to contribute fully.

- You keep your attention and focus on the Yonder Star for the meeting or interaction and engage in the dialogue looking from "What is missing?" versus "What's wrong?"

- You are actively engaged in the process, participating, asking questions, listening to what others say, and reacting with flexibility and goodwill.

- If you get distracted, you notice, self-intervene, and bring your full attention back to the task at hand.

- You are listening newly and remaining open to other points of view or "truths."

- Your openness and receptivity causes others to be more participatory and engaged, increasing the quality of interaction and collaboration.

Case Study: Be Responsible for Creating Value

Dwight—Taming My File Cabinet

Within the first few of hours of a three weekend program I was heartsick with the realization that I was facing long weekends with a trainer who I felt was a jerk. At the first break, I garnered lots of agreement from other participants regarding my "valuable" insight and "we can do this better ourselves" attitude. After the break, my internal voice was still running rampant with judgment and criticism. Then a thought about *choice* flashed into my mind. In that moment, I could choose to either continue suffering and complaining or to create and own a powerful stand for myself regarding the value I would get from my participation in the program. Here was a defining Leadership Choice Point moment, an opportunity for Self-Generated Accountability.

By being willing to self-observe, I discovered that my unhappiness was coming from unconscious and automatic comparisons with unpleasant childhood experiences. Although I didn't have the concept of our File Cabinet minds at the time, that is exactly where my internal dialogue was coming from! Once discovered, I recognized that it was my issue, not his, that his style had triggered something for me. Although I still didn't like the way the trainer worked, forming judgments based on my filters had been preventing any learning. I was actually wasting my own time being caught up in my judgments triggered by my historical filters. When I separated my filtered view of the trainer's performance and style from the content and value of the experience, I was able to set that internal dialogue aside, be mostly present in the course, and create extraordinary and lasting value from the course. One of my most important outcomes of that program was the creation of this Operating Principle, *Be Responsible For Creating Value*, which I now emphasize in every client engagement and in my own interactions in life.

Case Study: Be Responsible for Creating Value

Who's Bringing the Value?

A newer member of our business executive roundtable group shared that he was planning to leave the group because he didn't think he was getting enough value. He wanted to work on "meaty" business issues, provide vigorous challenge to each other's perspectives, help support each other, and keep focused on accomplishing strategic objectives. During the dialogue that followed, he began to hear from the other members that they wanted the same things. He also realized that he had not really been fully participating in the group's discussions, had missed meetings, arrived late or left early, and had not been bringing his own issues for discussion.

Since the group had arrived at a mutual Yonder Star for group experience and value, I asked: "What's missing?" Top on the list was *full* participation by *all* members, including attendance, frank interactions and bringing "A" issues and topics to discuss. These strategic challenges and opportunities, if they were resolved, would really make a difference in their business success, the quality of their lives, and the lives of those around them. They all started laughing when they looked around the room and asked each other, "Who goes first?" All of the group members began to see that they had become too casual in their participation. They made a new commitment to come to the group meeting having prepared in advance to bring their "A" issues for discussion. Imagine how the quality of the meetings improved when each member brought his or her presence and participation in this way.

This is the crux of this operating principle. Lead with your own participation in a way that you believe will create value and will invite others to do the same. So it begins with you…you go first. Bring intention, participation, and contribution—listening and speaking in a way that sets up a valuable environment and gives you value in return.

Practice Opportunities:
Be Responsible for Creating Value

Bring Attention to Your Intention

Flex your intention muscles and practice in these situations:

- A meeting you have called or a meeting you have been asked to attend
- A presentation or other setting where you are attending primarily at the request of another person and it is not your first choice
- In a conversation with another person where you historically get triggered into criticism

Think about your participation, its impact on others, and the value of the experience and ask yourself:

- How can I "show up" to bring high value?
- How can I prepare for the encounter so that I engage productively and curiously?
- What historical biases might get in my way?
- What Yonder Star can I create that is bigger than my historical bias?

Bring your "value creation" self to the event and participate fully. Afterwards ask yourself:

- What value did I create in each situation? For myself? Others? The presenter or meeting facilitator?
- What difference did it make to the meeting outcome, the presenter, or my associates?

For more support, check the Practical Applications—Section Five under: *Productive Meetings—Increasing Engagement and Outcomes.*

Operating Principle #8:

Make it Safe *and* Productive

When you take on this Operating Principle, you will be engaged in creating a safe environment where productivity can flourish. As in other sections of this book, we have joined together two words in one principle that aren't generally used together regarding conversations. You may think that conversations can either be safe *or* they can be productive—or at least you find it difficult to have both present. We are purposefully challenging that thinking and suggesting that the most powerful environment for raising and resolving issues productively is a safe one.

Mutual Trust, Respect, and Safety

> **Safety:** *the condition of being protected from or unlikely to cause danger, risk, or injury.*

The following image was used in Section One—Essential Notions to define and discuss Yonder Star and Vision-Focused Leadership, with a short reference to a Productive Environment as the foundation for team member collaboration. This Operating Principle, *Make it Safe and Productive*, underscores the critical component of safety in creating a firm foundation upon which to build collaboration. For participants in a conversation to be willing to fully engage, they must feel that they will be respected and their ideas heard rather than discounted, taken out of context, or later used against them.

Vision Focused Leadership

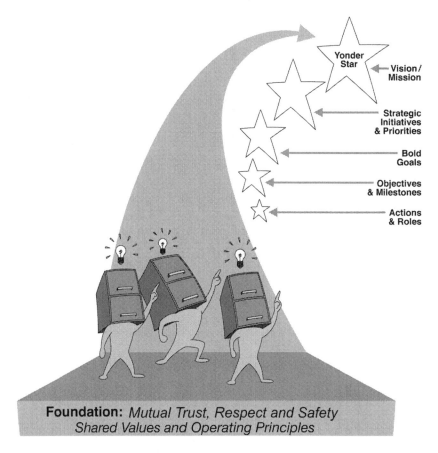

Foundation: *Mutual Trust, Respect and Safety*
Shared Values and Operating Principles

When full engagement involves personal sharing, this Operating Principle becomes especially important, since sharing genuinely involves a certain amount of vulnerability. Participants are revealing a part of themselves, their thoughts, feelings, past experiences, and even their filters. In order to really "explore truths" with others, an environment of mutual trust, respect, and safety is vital. The payoff is that the resulting environment encourages freewheeling creative interactions that lead to the most dynamic collaborations and productive outcomes.

How do you know when the participants consider an environment "safe"? Since you can't feel other people's feelings, you need only check your own—if you are hesitating about sharing something that you feel is relevant, then it isn't safe for you *or* others.

How Can You Make it Safe?

There are a number of the Operating Principles that, when employed, contribute to creating a safe environment. Designing personalized practices for yourself and your teams based on these principles will make them real in your conversations and meetings. Operating Principle #4, *Declare There is Nothing Wrong or Broken Here and Now*, instantly shifts your listening and the sense of safety experienced by others around you. Operating Principle #5, *Explore truths: Mine, Theirs, and Ours*, provides a context in which your interest is expressed and others feel their truths validated.

For meetings requiring creativity, problem solving, new directions, or new expressions of leadership, authentically declaring that each person's contributions are valid and valuable will dramatically raise the level and quality of ideas and participation. As the conversation unfolds, it may become safe enough for participants to float out "half-baked" or seemingly "dumb" ideas. These in turn may develop into great ideas or spark someone else to have a great idea. A couple of the best ideas we've seen developed in leadership team meetings were actually the result of someone misunderstanding another person's comment, restating it the way he or she heard it, and sparking the insight of the day!

Build on the Participation of Others

Another important step in creating a safe *and* productive atmosphere is to build on the participation engendered by this new feeling of mutual trust, respect, and safety in the group. Many times interactions in a group resemble a wheel with spokes—everyone is talking to the center hub (the meeting leader or other authority figure) and trying to score by making their points, rather than really listening to each other's input and building on each scenario offered before transitioning to a new point.

> Suzanne's family had the "dishtowel story" to use when it seemed that everyone was interrupting and not listening. The person originally telling the story would shift to telling a fictitious story—the dishtowel story—and ramble on until someone or everyone noticed! It was always about the dishtowels that didn't match and had to be returned to the store and the receipt couldn't be found and so on. Eventually everyone else at the table or in the room got the joke and turned their attention back to the speaker.

A version of this happens even in a friendly, personal conversation if you are too busy trying to formulate your points or responses to really listen to what the other is saying. By listening newly, being slow to understand, encouraging others to participate, and making sure your meaning lands correctly, you will facilitate more meaningful conversations, new opportunities and outcomes, and greater satisfaction in your interactions.

Safe *and* Productive = Direct *and* Sensitive

> ***Direct:*** *going straight to the point; frank*

> ***Sensitive:*** *having or displaying a quick and delicate appreciation of others' feelings*

Another important capacity for creating a safe *and* productive environment is to be both direct and sensitive. You may be wondering what we were thinking when we put those two ideas in the same sentence. Many of our clients do when they first encounter it.

By direct, we mean being frank, free, forthright, straightforward, and sincere in expression—no "beating around the bush," innuendos, or guessing games. Obviously, interpretations of being direct vary with the individual and even the geographic area. For example, when Dwight, a "Yankee," lived in Florida, he was sometimes seen as rude by long time residents of the area. No one would ever call him that (that would be rude); they'd just say something to the effect of "Yankees are rude…" Another interpretation of "direct" that seems to prevail with some folks is to consciously or subconsciously equate "direct" with "brutal." We do not intend either of those perspectives, which is why we include the word "sensitive" in the same phrase.

We use the word "sensitive" intentionally to be a bit provocative. We want to engage your brain and stimulate you to upgrade your thinking processes. We know "direct" has some pretty strong interpretations for some of our readers and also realize that "sensitive" can be heard as wimpy, weak, soft, or worse by some. By "sensitive," we mean highly aware of the attitudes and feelings of others.

Connecting back to our Productive Dialogue Zone two-circle diagram (displayed again on the next page) the middle area, where the top and bottom circles intersect, is both safe *and* productive and includes both direct and sensitive interaction and thought processes. Productive Dialogues require both a results focus (productivity) *and* a relationships focus (safety). The top Social Safety circle in the diagram represents sensitive, relationship-focused communication without dealing with real issues. Safety wins with no results. The bottom circle represents direct, Transaction Based communication without sensitivity to another's perspectives or contributions. Results achieved at the expense of safety, threaten the quality and longevity of the results and the relationships.

The Productive Dialogue Zone

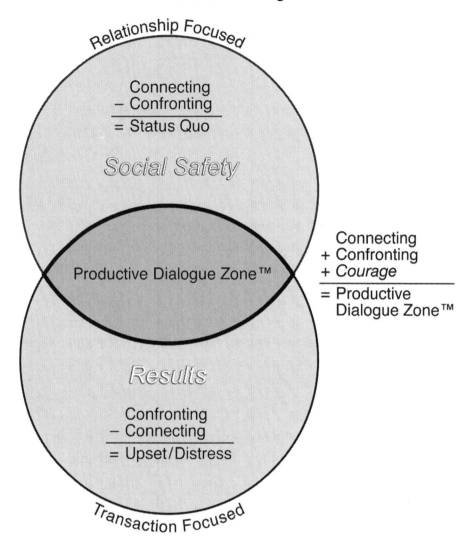

The capacity to be both direct and sensitive is essential to engaging effectively in conversations that deal with tough issues and still keep participants light and creatively engaged and collaborating. It is the essential component of the Productive Dialogue Zone and your individual and group's capacity to tackle and resolve issues effectively. The juxtaposition of "direct" *and* "sensitive," like "safe" *and* "productive," is intended to emphasize the multidimensional nature of the capacities in play in the Productive Dialogue Zone and the requirement for a *range* of abilities to get and stay connected while engaging in challenging or confronting conversations.

If you have been one who is very direct, you may not have noticed how many times your counterpart is reluctant to engage fully, agrees with everything you say, or ignores your request in a passive aggressive manner. In fact, if you have been overly proud of how direct you are, you may be shocked for a while when you upgrade your operating system, start being more open to your counterparts, and they open up to you. Be sure you have a few minutes and are sitting down. The conversational muscle for being direct that you have developed so far is an important capacity. It is most effective when combined with some awareness and sensitivity to how your "directness" is landing or affecting other's ability to be effective. You probably don't have to consciously exercise your "direct" muscle much more; for you it is a self-sustaining method of exercise. So instead, work on building muscle in the area of noticing your impact on others, how well you are connecting, and whether you are really getting what you want.

On the other hand, if you have considered yourself the "sensitive one," you may be quite excited when you upgrade and start being more direct. Be prepared for your counterparts to be surprised or even shocked—perhaps you could invite *them* to sit down. Depending on how little directness you have practiced in the past, it may take you awhile to calibrate your approach. After all, you have a well-developed "sensitivity" muscle, and it will take some regular exercising of your "direct muscle" to build it up to the level required for some conversations. To twist an old phrase, "Be direct and beg for forgiveness!" Be fearless and trust your highly developed sensitive muscle to alert you when it might not have landed the way you intended. Be responsible for what gets heard and you'll get the hang of it.

Why Is Making It Safe and Productive Important?

The open exchange of ideas that facilitates developing solutions, action, and movement toward your Yonder Star is created *only* in an atmosphere where participants are not afraid to speak up. When other participants in the discussion feel that what they say is valued and that they will not be subject to ridicule, they will most likely relax and start to tap into their creative energies. The creative, thinking, analytic part of our brain cannot be readily accessed when we are in fear. With waste and friction minimized, conversations and interactions can take a direct path toward resolving issues and fulfilling the Yonder Star.

What Difference Does It Make?

Invoking this Operating Principle of making it safe *and* productive for others and yourself creates a situation where you can expand your own and others' conversational capacities. The range of possible conversations increases exponentially when you find yourself in a situation where you can be direct and open and, at the same time, present to whether the other party is engaged in your interaction. That, in turn, will expand access to creativity and productive outcomes. You will find that you can develop yourself to be a person around whom *any* issue can be raised and resolved productively.

When Making it Safe and Productive Is Missing:

- You and others hesitate to really share your view, or tend to speak in a politically correct manner. Ego protection, reputation, or career safety is at the top of your awareness.

- In a group setting, members take shots at each other, using sarcasm or humor to score points and assert their own dominance, and consider direct and aggressive confrontation of others as "honest," right and perhaps even "heroic."

- You may see nonverbal cues such as looking upward, zombie nodding to appease.

- The really tough issues that need to be tackled are avoided because no one wants to be responsible for bringing them up and taking heat.

- After the meeting, everyone else hears primarily about the comments or emotions that took place inside the room—usually in a diminishing and gossipy manner.

When This Principle Is in Play:

- You set your own frame of mind productively, declaring each person's contribution is valid and valuable.

- You use "I" statements, signaling that you are owning your perceptions and ideas.

- If you normally try to avoid sensitive subjects, you now look for ways to be direct and deal with them in a productive manner.

- If you normally speed in with direct frontal attacks, you stop, shift your focus back to the Yonder Star, and ask, "What's missing?"

- You can see or feel the energy as participants lean forward to hear and concentrate on what is being said.

- People are puzzling, questioning, considering, and totally engaged in the process.

- When you speak on a topic that has had some emotional energy for you, you are able to speak about it calmly, rather than speaking *from* your emotions.

Case Study: Make it Safe *and* Productive

From Competitive to Effective

In the early days George was fortunate to have strong venture capital support for his business and was able to hire a full staff of highly talented executives. As the early leadership team struggled with creating and executing a powerful and effective strategy, competition among members of this talented group, none of whom had ever worked together, became increasingly intense. While each leader was doing an excellent job within his or her own group, communication was largely vertical in the organization. There were few processes that facilitated working effectively across the organization and little interest in or support for changing that situation. It was definitely not a safe environment. Sometimes it seemed that the executives would rather quietly beat each other than have their stock options pay off! Here was a case of having a collection of great intellectual capital with a challenge to create great collaborative capital.

George was a big believer in investing in leadership development and held regular offsite workshops and planning sessions. The team learned, adopted, and regularly talked about the Operating Principles. They explored how the ideas might expand their effectiveness and were willing to be accountable for their regular application. They learned to create an atmosphere of mutual trust, respect, and safety in which they could raise and resolve issues productively. They took on the challenge of having results *and* a collaborative relationship.

A few of the initial leadership team members didn't make it as rapid growth continued and collaboration became a much higher priority. The balance of the executives became a very effective unit that could address issues directly and move to solutions and action. George credits this collaborative leadership team with the firm's rapid growth and successful public offering.

Case Study: Make it Safe *and* Productive

Dwight—Let It In and Learn

For about five years in his later life, my dad would not speak to me or have anything to do with me. I made periodic efforts at communicating, got discouraged, and had pretty much given up. With Suzanne's coaching I created a Yonder Star of a great, loving, and functional relationship with my dad and began to look and listen for opportunities. The opportunity presented itself as my daughter's wedding day approached and we would all be in the same place at the same time. After we arrived, I arranged to meet privately in my parents' hotel room. My dad didn't say anything for a long time, just continued to watch TV. I finally said, "I guess there are some things you have wanted to tell me for a long time…"

Eventually he started and soon was on a roll. Most of the things he shared I either didn't remember the same way or certainly had a very different perspective on the events. It took all I had to keep quiet, listen, keep displacing unproductive thoughts, and be present without defense or justification. I found it extremely difficult and yet knew that any hope of success hinged on my ability to truly listen with no resistance or argument—to make it safe enough for my dad to fully unload. Focusing on my Yonder Star of a great, loving, and functional relationship with my dad displaced the importance of proving that my remembrance of these events was the right one.

After that interaction we were reasonably sociable with each other for the wedding period, and within a few months, my parents traveled to our home for an extended visit. By using everything I could muster, displacing defense with a more powerful Yonder Star, I had made it safe enough for my dad to be completely open and let go of past upsets, some of which he had been carrying around for decades. Our relationship grew rapidly and steadily better from there on for the rest of his life.

Practice Opportunities:
Make it Safe *and* Productive

Pick Your Scenario and Get to Work!

Here is an opportunity to pick an area of development that will help leverage your leadership. Whether you feel you have been one to be overly direct, missing the sensitive side or one who has been reluctant to rock the boat, there is a practice for you.

Scenario #1: If you have been **very direct in the past** or intensely focused on the transaction and the results, you probably missed the sensitive, connected, relationship side. You could practice making it safer to interact with you! Pick a person and a scenario you would like to see resolved.

- Have a new conversation with that person where you share your intention to brainstorm possible solutions together and to resolve the issue in a way that works for both of you.
- Cause connection by using Exploration Listening; other-focused, intentionally listening for their content, feelings and higher intention.
- Assure the person that you are very interested in his or her perspective and the well-being of everyone involved.

Since you have historically been directive and transactional, you may have to spend some time getting them comfortable that you are not just kidding or setting them up for something. This part will be a test of your ability to bring authenticity and to build trust.

Scenario #2: If you have been overly careful, sensitive, or **reluctant to bring things up** for fear of loss of esteem or of hurting another's feelings, you have probably missed many opportunities for speaking up for results. In keeping quiet or preventing "rocking the boat," you may have been sacrificing productivity for personal safety. It's not either/or—it's both! You could add a higher degree of productivity to the safety you create. Pick a person and a scenario you would like to see resolved. If you need a shot of courage or daring to continue, make a list of the potential consequences if the issue is not addressed or resolved.

- Craft a clear statement of the issue from your perspective (separate from the person), what your part in it is, and your ideal outcome.
- Once you feel confident that there is no shame, blame, or judgment in your statement, share it with him or her.
- Share your feelings about the importance of working it through and ask if the person would be willing to engage in a resolution conversation with you.
- Emphasize that it is important to you to understand his or her perspective on the issue and for the two of you to work together to reach a solution that works for both of you.

Since you have historically been reluctant, overly sensitive, or may have avoided bringing up tough issues, others may be surprised by your new, bolder conversations. That's OK, they will get used to it! Increase the stakes by getting vulnerable and let others know you are working on speaking up and weighing in on important issues rather than letting them stack up in silence.

Scenario #3: If you tend to **interrupt** or can't wait to add in your brilliant input, others may feel dismissed or disregarded. You could increase safety and productivity around you!

- Consider carrying a small notebook around and jot down your thoughts and ideas briefly, rather than interrupting. If you practice this, be sure to get permission from whomever you are with and be sure that it is not distracting for them. Also, watch yourself to be sure you are not avoiding being present by hiding in your notebook.
- Focus and listen fully to what the other person is saying. Exploration Listening works well here to create a connection.
- See if you can build on their idea—a real test of your full creative engagement—waiting to add your suggestion until that idea has run its course.

Get vulnerable—share with people around you that you are working on contributing in a highly productive manner and you have found a way to save up your idea bursts and present them at more appropriate times. If you are a person who tends to interrupt, believe me, they all know it about you already! This is a demonstration of Self-Generated Accountability—you are managing yourself to get and bring value.

Scenario #4: If you have a **reputation for killing the messenger**, or retaliation, it is definitely *not* a safe or productive environment around you. You have trained people to avoid or dilute bad news or wait until they have solved a significant issue before updating you. You could retrain your environment to interact with you in a much more current and heads-up manner, keeping it safe and productive to deal with real data in a timely manner.

- Let your staff know that you have realized that "killing the messenger" is an obvious block to getting important and timely information.
- Let them know you are committing yourself to dealing with real issues and will personally take responsibility for your own reactions to unpleasant news.
- Give them permission to call you on it if you don't!
- When you receive the next "bad news," breathe—especially breathe out—before saying anything.
- Move immediately to clarifying questions (watch yourself on slipping into interrogation mode), to help you understand rather than react to the news and give you time to cool off.

Be Responsible for What Gets Heard

That's not what I meant!

Misunderstandings are a key factor in causing friction and waste in human interactions, and they are much more common than you might like to admit. An important aspect of leadership effectiveness is being able to have things happen through, and be successfully produced by others. Your ability to move others into appropriate, timely, and effective action is largely determined by the consequences of your speaking and listening. When you take ownership of how your communication landed with the other people you will naturally move to clarifying dialogue as a means to move the topic, conversation, and relationship forward. When you take ownership of your own listening—what you heard—you will be a more objective and engaged listener.

The central message of this Operating Principle is that, if you intend to be an effective leader, particularly in the face of fear, resistance, and unrelenting change, 100% ownership for mutual understanding of the content and context of your conversations is on you!

Remember the term Self-Generated Accountability and the relevant discussion about what you are actually in control of in any moment, conversation or relationship? You have control (whether you exercise it or not) over your own thinking, listening, and speaking. Of course you cannot take control of another person's filters or understanding. You can, however, be present, curious, and responsive to how your communications are touching the three levels of conversational impact—the topic, the conversation, and the relationship—and put in the necessary correction so that what you mean is what is understood.

In taking responsibility for what gets heard, you will not simply be limiting this principle to what you say. Often what you don't say, your body language, underlying tone, errors of omission rather than commission, and the way you are listening is as powerful as or more so than what you do say. For some specific application recommendations see the Practical Applications Section Five: *Project Performance Review – Achieving Clarity and Alignment*.

What You Say Impacts How You Are Heard

"Quote me as saying I was misquoted."

Groucho Marx–*American Comedian and Film Star*

There are a number of common pitfalls that set up misunderstanding in the conversation. It often takes a trained and objective third-party view to make you aware of some of the ones you most commonly fall into and of your most entrenched habits. The more power you have in an organization or in a situation, the less feedback you will get from those around you about what works and what doesn't work in your communications. Remember as you take on this material, it is for your own development, not for your unsolicited advice to others!

Disconnected Speaking—Monologues

Some CEOs and key executives that we work with through coaching or in our groups have the disease of using lots of words to make their point. Listeners (usually subordinates) nod (sometimes nod off), get disconnected from what is being said, or simply get lost in the lengthy, obtuse description. Zig Ziglar says, "Be a meaningful specific, not a wandering generality."

If this is one of your areas for development, practice getting clear about the intention, context, and main or key pieces of the content of your message. If your tendency is to wander into multiple territories in your conversations (similar to having lots of windows open on your computer desktop), work on sticking to fully completing one topic before moving to the next. These actions will help make it easier for others to get on the same page with you. Work on removing barriers to communication and understanding caused by your own speaking.

Interpretations of Interpretations

One of the most unproductive outcomes of communication is the proliferation of interpretations of what was said.

You have probably been part of one or more of those conversations where, after the meeting, participants share their interpretations of what they think someone meant during the meeting and then debate their interpretations with each other, rather than get clarity from the source on exactly what was meant. The outcome is like playing the old game of "telephone," where the end message doesn't sound anything like the original. Are you relying on multiple levels of interpretation or are you communicating directly for clarity?

Be conscious and learn who around you is considered to be your interpreter. It may not be the specific responsible party you have designated. Who are people asking if they are not sure what you meant if they are not asking you? Is that what you want? If it is, be sure that your interpreter is very clear and check in with him or her often. If it is not what you want, what does the practice say about your own approachability?

Sending Others to Survival Brain Mode

Another pitfall in your communication that disconnects others and sends them into their own File Cabinet or survival brain mode occurs when your speaking carries with it your unproductive emotions. There is a huge difference between being frustrated, recognizing that you are frustrated, and even talking *about* your frustration, and actually speaking while you are feeling frustrated. When you speak while experiencing your own unproductive emotions, what comes across louder than your words is the emotion. Other people's brains immediately go to survival thinking or make stuff up about what your emotions mean about them (first) or the situation.

Besides closing off the creative parts of their brain, their reaction also interferes with their ability to hear the content of the message. Susan Scott's wise counsel offered in her trainings and her book *Fierce Conversations* is "Be Responsible for Your Emotional Wake." What is the emotional wake around you? Is it what you intend? Are you even aware of the ripple effect?

> During one of Suzanne's resource speaker assignments, she encountered a CEO group member who challenged this notion rather vehemently. The member asserted that when she yells and screams at her executives, and they slink off to their offices, she knows for sure that they got the message and its importance. If this comment feels comfortable to you, consider the kind of team you are actually building. People who will put up with that type of abuse, over time, are probably those who adapted to that kind of treatment early in life and have learned to appease to survive, or may be people who have no other choices for another form of employment. Those who want to contribute their creativity and initiative will leave as soon as they have the opportunity. That leaves you with a group of appeasing, survival-brain-driven employees waiting to be told what to do and hesitant to take any risk at all for fear of retribution.

There are potentially many habits to catch in your speaking that tend to send other people to their survival brain. Speaking from your negative emotions is certainly a key factor to catch. Other simple shifts such as replacing the word "but" with "and" and replacing "should" with "could" will lighten up a perception by the recipient of being judged or discounted. While these two simple recommendations are not new, they are really not very widely embraced. To be effective, your speaking has to be combined with a shift in your framework of thinking rather than occur just as a word-processing "search and replace" in your language. Remember speaking *follows* your frame of thinking. See the Practical Applications—Section Five: *Eliminate the Buts* for some examples.

How You Listen Impacts What Gets Heard

> *To listen well is as powerful a means of influence as to talk well and is essential to all true conversation.*

> **Chinese Proverb**

The way you speak to another person is not the only communication modality to consider when being responsible for what gets heard. The way you listen to another person has a huge influence on whether or not they hear *your* content and, most importantly, the context in which they hear it.

We have discussed, in earlier sections, the value of listening newly, being intentionally slow to understand, and declaring that each person's contribution is valid and valuable. These are elements of a valuable manner of listening—a valuable mind-set going into a conversation.

The Operating Principle interventions begin to stack up here and integrate together as we explore the Operating Principles in this last section on Productive Dialogue. Making it safe *and* productive and declaring there is nothing wrong or broken *here and now* are also incredibly important aspects of being responsible for what gets heard.

When another person senses that you authentically appreciate them and have an ear for what they are saying, you both get connected in the conversation and experience a sense of being on the same team. The way they interpret a subsequent communication from you, as a partner, is very different than the context provided for an adversary or someone from whom they must protect themselves, their reputation, or their ideas.

100% Responsibility as a Listener

Listening is a magnetic and strange thing, a creative force. Those who listen to us are the ones we move toward. When we are listened to, it creates us, makes us unfold and expand.

Unknown

When you are the listener, you are 100% responsible for what you heard. *Now wait a minute—didn't we just say, in several ways, that the speaker is responsible for what gets heard?* This operating principle applies when you are a listener also. It doesn't say the speaker is responsible or the listener is responsible; it says "be responsible (that's you) for what gets heard." It applies to *you* in each and every role you have in a conversation.

You don't get to use this on others as a defense, as in "You're supposed to be responsible for what I heard!" When you are listening to others, being responsible for what gets heard (by you) is an important method of focusing attention that displaces your preconceived notions and biases that could taint the context and content being delivered. Here we are, back to Self-Generated Accountability. So now, when you hear multiple, and often conflicting, interpretations of a communication that is pertinent to you or your work, what is your responsibility? Check out and clarify what you heard and how it applies, and ask any clarifying questions that will help you.

What You Don't Say Impacts How You Are Heard

Avoidance and Appeasing

Are you one of the people who think maybe it is just better to avoid the issue all together? Avoidance sends a message about your leadership that speaks very loudly. It impacts your credibility and your leadership reputation. Another way that what you *don't* say affects how you are heard is excessive dancing around a topic or political correctness gone berserk.

While talking about the topic is much better than overt avoidance, it is important to be able to speak directly to the issue at hand. When you have developed a reputation for hiding meaning in long obtuse, circuitous, or gratuitous sentences, you are heard through a filter of insincerity or mistrust. That has people label *you* as insincere or untrustworthy.

Your emotions speak louder than your words, and a conflicting context for your communication will betray the best planned content. Remember to confront and deal with real issues by being both direct *and* sensitive to make it safe *and* productive!

Body Language

One type of nonverbal feedback is your listener's body language. If your listeners start demonstrating that they are closing up by crossing their arms, sitting back, or turning their chairs or bodies away from you, you have probably hit a nerve or said something they have found disagreeable. If they start leaning forward, look you in the eye, or nod their heads, they are connecting with something you've said. We don't address body language any more specifically here, except to point out that it flows naturally and is a consequence of your thinking or "where you are coming from."

Your perseverance in reading this book to this point demonstrates your commitment to learning to work with underlying, real issues. The Operating Principles are designed to cause interventions in your thinking, so allow them to flow through you and be present to the body language you observe as you speak. If the incoming data is not consistent with your intention and is not demonstrating Productive Dialogue ask yourself, "What are they hearing or experiencing from me?" Ask questions as discussed below. Listen newly and be slow to understand. Shift your thinking to a productive mode and start again. Connecting and welcoming body language will flow from your shift in mental framework.

If you are interested in developing your skills at reading body language, there are lots of books and trainings available on the subject, particularly on negotiation and in sales training programs.

How Do I Know *What* is Being Heard?

Ask Questions

You don't get to assume that others are hearing and interpreting your communication the way you mean it. To get certainty, ask probing questions arising from genuine curiosity. Pay close attention to the feedback, both verbal and nonverbal, and alter your speaking style, direction, or message for better results. Stay with it until you are clearly connecting.

You may be thinking, "Wow, sometimes it's hard enough just to figure out what to say…now I have to be able to figure out if people are hearing it correctly, too." This is not as difficult as it may seem. After you speak, pause and then ask a few short, probing questions, such as "What's your take on this?" "What are you hearing here?" or "How do you see this playing out?" We have provided a list of additional questions in the Practice Opportunity at the end of this principle. Make sure your questions are producing much more than simple yes-or-no answers. If you don't, what you're likely to get back is an automatic "yes" that has nothing to do with comprehension and more to do with not wanting to look stupid, inattentive, or uncooperative.

You are particularly susceptible to this type of response if your approach has a bit of "the grand inquisitor" in it. If you frequently fall into this trap, spend time and energy getting comfortable with yourself and your willingness to be open to whatever comes back from your questions. Inquisitions are generally driven by domination, control, and protecting yourself. You will find a number of Operating Principles missing in your expression. Very few people enjoy being grilled. Also, they can generally tell whether you really care about their answers or are just going through the motions because you have read our book and it seemed like a good idea. Remember what Dwight's mom always said, "It's all in your tone of voice!"

Get Comfortable with Silence

After you have asked your question, be quiet! Leave room and time for processing and for a thoughtful answer—or clarifying questions. To ask, "Got that? … OK, good!" is not an example of asking open-ended questions and then waiting for answers. You may be thinking, "That is going to take a lot of time! How can I afford that?" Can you afford rework, do-overs, missed deadlines, and defensiveness that can occur due to misunderstanding regarding your motives or intention?

Why Is Being Responsible for What Gets Heard Important?

In our view you can't get close to Self-Generated Accountability without fully owning this Operating Principle. To live your life or to interact with others without it leaves you a victim to your filters and those of others. Step beyond being a source of waste and drama. Take responsibility for the ripple effect around you and be sure you are sending out productive waves with the impact that you intend to send. If you seriously intend to send damaging waves, stop reading this book and go get therapy—it's all about you. When the waves crash onshore differently than you intended, cleaning it up is being an emotionally mature adult—take it on.

If you notice that your communications tend to land the same way with a certain person over and over, examine your role in that outcome and have conversations with them for increasing your capacities together. You can develop your capacities for Productive Dialogue together. You will find an example of this kind of conversation in the Practical Applications—Section Five: *Have a Conversation About Your Conversations: Building Conversational Capacities.*

What Difference Does It Make?

The feedback you gain will help guarantee that the person or group you are working with doesn't walk away from the conversation with different versions of what went on, what was agreed upon, and the actions to be taken. By holding yourself accountable for what gets heard, you are also partnering with the other person or group in what gets done—more of that Self-Generated Accountability at work. You will gain a reputation as a clear communicator. Your conversational capacities will increase, and you will gain effectiveness in your team for handling even complex situations.

When Being Responsible for What Gets Heard Is Missing:

- You justify your emotions and consider those reasons as justification for communicating while in your emotions.

- You think other people should just learn to understand you, or you use your personality type or theirs as an excuse for the way you interact.

- You simply think you are right and others are wrong or just wimps.

- You accept cultural stereotypes as an explanation for your ineffective communication.

- People often walk away from the conversation with confused or mistaken interpretations of what is expected of them or of what will be happening next.

When This Principle Is in Play:

- You communicate with intention, encourage questions, and your communication is an interaction rather than a monologue.

- You are more direct, doing less talking around a point and more talking to the point.

- You take time up front to help ensure clarity and underlying intent of the message.

- You remove barbs, hooks, and other triggering words and negative tones before communicating.

- You ask situation-appropriate questions such as, "How is this landing over there?", "What are you hearing?"

- You can speak about your emotions rather than speaking while in your unproductive emotions.

- People are comfortable asking you clarifying questions and consider you approachable.

Case Study:
Be Responsible for What Gets Heard

Be Right or Be Effective

Paul, was presenting his topic during an executive meeting and was not connecting very well with the other participants. When questioned about what he thought was not working in the conversation, he made several unsuccessful attempts to convince us of his perspective. Finally he exclaimed, "Look, I have spent many years learning to say exactly what I mean, clearly and distinctly. If the other executives can't get it, it's their problem." He wasn't kidding when he said it! Paul had a rough time with the group that day. His boss and peers did not have to put up with his arrogant perspective the way his employees presumably had to, and they didn't.

Paul got the message and after that impactful day he worked hard at giving up his right to be unilateral in his speaking. He has learned to check out what is getting heard and to interact in an open way. He stays with the conversation until he is clear that what he is intending with his communication and what others are hearing matches up. Not surprisingly, his career has blossomed as well. Imagine the opportunities for productivity gains in Paul's operations over time as he learned to shift from monologues with his people to dialogues and to check to see what they were actually hearing.

Practice Opportunities: Be Responsible for What Gets Heard

Practice #1: Communicate with a Clean and Clear Intention

A clear intention is usually conscious and includes a delivery method that considers recipient understanding. A clean intention is one that moves things forward without hooks, barbs, judgments, or tones of voice that send people into survival brain mode. Ask yourself these questions before communicating:

- What are the message (content) and context I intend to deliver?
- What emotion might get in my own way?
- What language or tone have I used in the past that could be distracting or send people into their survival brain?
- Do I use swear words or other questionable references that I think are no big deal, yet might trigger others?
- Who can I ask about my blind spots, triggering words, and tones in my communication?
- What biases or historical perspective might the listeners have?
- How can I communicate effectively if those biases are present?

Practice #2: Check How the Message Landed

In your next conversation or meeting, use these questions to get feedback that will help you understand how the message was received. Being responsible for what gets heard means you give up the right to blame the other person for their misunderstanding. Clear it up and clean it up!

- My intention has been to…How am I doing?
- What else would help clarify the assignment? What can I add more detail about?
- What do you see as the most difficult part of this assignment?
- How can we be sure we stay on the same page/keep each other updated on progress?
- What is your understanding of the scope of the project/solution we've come up with?
- What is your take-away from this conversation?
- How will you summarize this for others?
- Please tell me what you are hearing.
- How is this landing over there?
- What aspect of the project can I provide more clarity about?
- What is your sense of the level of difficulty of this request/resolution/proposed action?
- Are there other priorities that will slip because of this request?
- What part do you expect me to contribute?
- What part of this will require more support or resources?
- What level of resources do you anticipate using for this?
- Are there any roadblocks you can already see?
- What could knock this project completely sideways?
- How has what I've said affected your thoughts/feelings?

Practical Applications— Conversational Examples & Tools

In this section, we explore the "how to" of applying the Operating Principles and Essential Notions. We have combed through feedback from our clients regarding their most pressing concerns and we have chosen a few common leadership challenges and provided you with an approach that applies the ideas and practices in this book.

Always important and yet often elusive, the ability to address the kinds of basic issues presented here is rapidly becoming even more essential for leaders. As the pace of change quickens and the level of uncertainty rises, the capacity to raise and resolve issues productively and quickly and have regular, reliable access to a variety of perspectives and interpretations will make the difference between success and failure.

Comfort with identifying and clearing upsets, first in yourself and then in others, will determine whether you are able to lead collaboratively based on a shared Yonder Star or must resort to the traditional command and control mindset. Learning to listen in a way that keeps you present and connected while continuing to forward the action will give you a much clearer view of what is going on around you. In addition, it will facilitate the free flow of information and allow you and your team to be much more present and in touch as the new rules of the game are created and evolve.

As you read through each of these conversational examples, challenge yourself to choose a person in your life for whom this type of conversation is appropriate and work with it! For more support, check our Web site at www.2130partners.com for more tools and programs.

The Three Levels of Conversational Impact as a Diagnostic Tool

After working diligently to apply the Operating Principles and Essential Notions, are you still having trouble getting through some issues? Are there some people with whom it seems very difficult to establish an environment of mutual trust, respect and safety? Have you followed our advice when you or the other person is upset and stopped driving your agenda—and now you are wondering how you can ever get back to resolving the real issue? Most of the Practical Applications are examples of how to have productive conversations about certain topics or in specific situations. When those conversations still don't work, how can you know what level of conversation to have next?

Three Levels of Conversational Impact

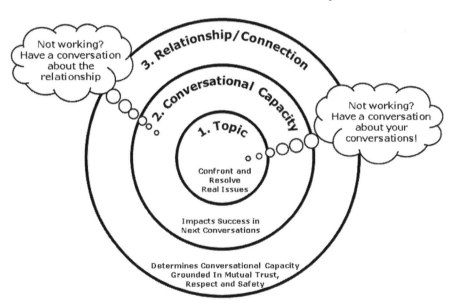

In the Essential Notions—Section One we presented four key ideas about what happens in every conversation:

- The conversation leaves an impact at the level of topic, conversational capacity, and relationship.

- The topic is resolved, stalled, or set back.

- Conversational capacities are enhanced, flat-lined, or decreased.

- Relationships are either built up or torn down.

Use the Three Levels of Conversational Impact as a diagnostic. If it isn't working at the level of topic resolution, stop talking about the topic and have a conversation about your conversations. If that doesn't work, have a conversation about your relationship. With that diagnosis, the next two applications address the "how to."

The success of these conversations is predicated on your ability and willingness to have a rigorous conversation with yourself—examine your own truths, be vulnerable, and be courageous.

Have a Conversation about Your Conversations— Building Capacities

Only when you are more committed to the success of a project or relationship than to your ego, getting credit, or being right will you be able to successfully build new collaborative capacities with another.

As you engage with others with your new knowledge, you will quickly discover that to increase the productivity of your daily interactions, rigorous, continuous practice is required. You must engage in challenging conversations to build conversational muscle. A key method to leverage your effectiveness is to learn to have a conversation with another about your conversations. In that exercise, treat your interactions themselves as fair game and fertile ground for your mutual learning and development. This is *not* a conversation for resolving a particular issue or problem. The topic for discussion in these conversations is enhancing the productivity and effectiveness of your interactions with each other. It is a method for building conversational capacity and relationship. Your conversations—including their successes and failures—are the primary focus.

Not every conversation hits the target of delivering maximum productivity while minimizing friction and waste. There is almost always room for improvement. By reviewing and working through the stumbling blocks in your conversations, you can usually significantly improve productivity. While you may find practice uncomfortable and sometimes discouraging, most learning and progress occurs from noticing and correcting small failures. Even physical trainers push you to muscle failure in your practice to build strength. If using this application doesn't work to restore mutual trust, respect, and safety, then perhaps "having a conversation about our relationship" is the next level for you to address.

The Operating Principles to consider while working through this application include:

> Principle #1: Be Present, Stay in the Game
>
> Principle #2: Listen Newly, Be Intentionally Slow to Understand
>
> Principle #3: Take Myself Lightly
>
> Principle #6: Confront and Deal with Real Issues

Follow the outline of how to proceed through a conversation about your conversations, including preparation before your conversation and key points to consider during the conversation:

Outline: Have a Conversation about Your Conversations
Building Conversational Capacities

Before the Conversation:

1. Identify a specific person with whom you are committed to having even more productive interactions. This could be a close personal acquaintance or a colleague, employee, boss, client, or vendor who is important to you, to the success of your work, or to producing desired project outcomes.

2. Clarify, for yourself, the Yonder Star you believe you share with the other person. If in doubt, invent one and discuss it as part of the conversation. (Examples: the success of a project, the ability to work together effectively, increased overall efficiencies or effectiveness in the team, etc.)

3. Identify your contribution to the current situation. Yes! You have a role! How is it that you could interact differently? Where have you been impeding the process?

Begin the Conversation:

1. Ask the other person if he or she would be willing to talk with you about how you two could be much more productive in your interactions. Use your own words; just be sure it comes across as an invitation! Some suggestions:

   - "John, would you be willing to have a conversation with me to explore how we might increase effectiveness in our work together?"

   - "John, that last conversation didn't work that well for me, and I suspect it didn't for you either. Can we talk about how we work together?"

2. Use "I" statements throughout!

3. Share your commitment to the relationship. If you are asking "What relationship?," go back to steps 1 and 2 above under "Before the Conversation." Here are some suggestions to help you get started:

   - "I am committed to having the kind of relationship with you that allows us to raise and resolve tough issues as efficiently as possible and where we are both treated with respect and dignity."

   - "It is my intention to develop the kind of working relationship with you that allows us to move through tough stuff quickly—and respectfully."

   - "I am committed to working in a collaborative manner with you, and I'd like to talk about how we can do that more effectively."

   - "I'm working on developing my leadership skills and the productivity of my conversations. Our conversations about XYZ project are a good place for me to practice, given our mutual responsibility for the outcomes."

   - "Our working relationship is an example to all of our direct reports, and I am committed to practicing what I advocate. There has got to be a way for us to get through tough issues without so much blood!"

4. Go first with sharing about your contribution to the current condition of your conversations and relationship. Share your thoughts about how you can improve your own participation. Some suggestions:

- "I know that I get impatient sometimes and check out…for our next conversation about XYZ project I will schedule it in advance and block the time slot we need."

- "I know that I get upset easily when I feel surprised by project progress issues, and that shuts down the conversation. I know that's my thing to work on, and I am going to work on having my surprised feeling be a cue for me to breathe and get present and curious."

- If appropriate, apologize for any impact or unintended consequences that may have occurred as a result of your past behavior.

5. Ask the other person how he or she thinks you could be more effective together.

    - "How could our conversations be more productive from your perspective?"

    - "What could I do differently?"

    - "What changes would you be willing to make?"

6. Be quiet, focus, and listen!

7. Make mutual commitments about how to have the next conversation about the issues or projects.

After the Conversation:

Check in to review, acknowledge improvement or breakdowns, and refresh as needed.

Worksheet: Have a Conversation About Your Conversations

1. Identify a specific person with whom you are committed to having even more productive interactions.

   _____

   _____

   _____

2. Clarify the Yonder Star you believe you share with the other person.

   _____

   _____

   _____

   _____

3. Identify your own contribution to the current situation. Where do you impede progress? Do you check out, dismiss, or get impatient? Are you unavailable? Preoccupied? Do you get upset easily?

   _____

   _____

   _____

   _____

   _____

4. What can you do differently? _Hint: Check all of the Operating Principles._

   _____

   _____

   _____

   _____

5. Engage in the conversation, keep what works, make some changes for increased effectiveness, and celebrate what works!

Have a Conversation about Your Relationship— Building Mutual Trust, Respect, and Safety

We have repeatedly stressed the importance of creating an environment of mutual trust, respect, and safety so that the most productive and collaborative work can be accomplished—particularly in conditions of fear, resistance, and unrelenting change. All of the Operating Principles, when applied diligently, support this notion. Nevertheless, there are certain conversations that just don't seem to work no matter what Operating Principle you practice. It could be that you are applying them with the best of intentions on top of a relationship where mutual trust, respect, or safety is missing or must be mended or revived. It is critical to continually build and mend relationships when necessary so that when you really need support and collaboration, they are there to draw from.

The Operating Principles to consider while working through this application are:

Principle #1: Be Present, Stay in the Game

Principle #2: Listen Newly, Be Intentionally Slow to Understand

Principle #3: Take Myself Lightly

Principle #8: Make It Safe *and* Productive

Principle #9: Be Responsible for What Gets Heard

Work through the following outline of how to proceed through a conversation about your relationship, including preparation work before your conversation and key points to consider during the conversation.

Outline: Have a Conversation about the Relationship
Building Mutual Trust, Respect and Safety

Before the Conversation:

1. Consider your relationship and the conversations you have had with the other person. What do you think is missing in the relationship? Is it mutual trust, respect, or safety?

2. What is missing for *you* in the relationship?

   - Do you feel safe to talk about whatever needs to be discussed?

   - Do you trust yourself to be able to be present, catch your unproductive emotions, and stay in the game?

   - Do you feel the other person respects your contribution?

3. What is missing in your regard for the other person?

   - Can you make it a safe environment for them to discuss what matters most? If not what is missing for you to be able to offer yourself that way?

   - Do you feel they share the same goal, values, or urgency?

4. What is the impact of your current relationship status? On you, them, the team, the goal?

5. What could happen if nothing changes in your relationship?

6. Clarify, for yourself, the Yonder Star you believe you share with the other person. If in doubt, invent one and discuss it as part of the conversation (examples: the success of a project, the ability to work together effectively, increased overall efficiencies or effectiveness in the team, ripple affect or example to others around you).

7. Identify your contribution to the current situation. Yes! You have a role! How is it that you could interact differently? Where have you been impeding the process?

8. What is an ideal outcome? If your conversation together alters the relationship significantly, what would be different?

9. Craft an opening statement that invites the other person into a conversation with you. Preparing your opening statement is intended to encourage you to be thoughtful and purposeful about it. See what negative emotions or old baggage comes up for you before going "live" with the other person. Don't over choreograph it or try to anticipate what the other person might say and all of your possible responses! Be clear in your opening statement or opening question that your intention is to enhance the relationship. This is not an opportunity to whine about how you don't feel safe or complain about their lack of cooperation!

Begin the Conversation:

1. Ask the other person if he or she would be willing to talk with you about how you two could be much more productive in your interactions and build the kind of relationship where even the toughest of issues can be raised and resolved. Use your own words; just be sure it comes across as an invitation! Some suggestions:

   ▪ "Joan, I'd like to build a much more productive working relationship with you, and I have reflected on some things I could do differently…would you be willing to discuss/ work on that with me?"

   ▪ "Joan, our working relationship is a role model to all the people who work for us, and my intention is to build it to a really productive level. Could we have a conversation to mend the fences/work through the issues that are getting in our way?"

2   Use 'I' statements throughout!

3. Share your commitment to the relationship and state what you see could be enhanced. Here are some suggestions to help you get started:

- "I am committed to having the kind of relationship where it is safe to raise tough issues and have confidence that we will work through them respectfully.

    o   "We used to have that and somewhere it went south."

    o   "The safety in our relationship to just say what is there to say and to work things out is not there for me; is it for you?"

    o   "What do we need to talk through or get past in order to restore a healthy working relationship?"

- "I intend to model the kinds of productive working relationships that I expect of those who work for me, and to that end I really would like to sort out between us what is not working."

    o   What happened—from your perspective—to get us off track?

    o   What can we learn from that episode that will help us now?

    o   Are there still misunderstandings from that situation that we could clear up to help us move forward?

4. Be big and go first with Self-Generated Accountability. Where can you take ownership or responsibility for the gaps and misunderstandings—authentically? Use your own words!

   ▪ "I can see that I have not been as forthcoming with information as I could be, and that has caused some issues between us."

   ▪ "I am sorry for any unproductive part I have played in our relationship; I've been in reaction mode for sure."

   ▪ "I haven't been supportive or even seemed very interested in the ideas you bring forward in executive meetings, and I am sure that has contributed to the distance in our relationship."

   ▪ "I have felt more competitive with you than cooperative, and I can see the damage that has caused."

5. Connect with a higher purpose for the relationship—what are the opportunities?

   ▪ "The (mutual goal) is really important and I can see that a new, more respectful, collegial relationship between us would take our focus and emotional energy off you and me and direct it to the issues to tackle together."

   ▪ "If we are really going to accomplish "X," it would be very helpful for us to find our way forward in our relationship because there are plenty of outside obstacles to work through together."

6. What is next?

   ▪ "Here are some things that I could do differently…and am willing to do differently"

- "What changes would you be willing to make?"

7. Make mutual commitments for follow-up and resolve what comes up next in the relationship. Anytime powerful people work together to accomplish big goals, there is a probability that relationship issues of mutual trust respect and safety come up. The idea isn't to avoid them; it is to be able to have confidence that you can talk about them and sort them out in a mutually satisfying manner.

   - "In our executive meetings, if I have an issue with the way we are interacting, I will say 'Can we chat briefly afterwards to clear up a few points?' rather than attack during the meeting—that could be our cue to each other."

   - "Let's schedule lunch once a month to stay on top of how we are doing and catch any slips before a wall gets built up."

   - "Let's get together after our schedules of meetings and presentations this week to connect and adjust a bit."

After the Conversation:

What went well? What did you learn for your next "relationship" conversation? Check in to review, acknowledge improvement or breakdowns, and refresh as needed.

Worksheet: Have a Conversation About the Relationship
Building Mutual Trust, Respect, and Safety

1. Identify the person with whom you are committed to having a more productive relationship.

   _____

   _____

2. Clarify the Yonder Star you believe you share with the other person.

   _____

   _____

3. Identify your own contribution to the current relationship situation.

   _____

   _____

   _____

4. What is an ideal outcome? If the relationship changes significantly after the conversation, what would be different?

   _____

   _____

   _____

5. What can you do differently? *Hint: Check all of the Operating Principles.*

   _____

   _____

6. Engage in the conversation, keep what works, make some changes for increased effectiveness and celebrate what works!

Questions to Explore Reality— Curiosity versus Interrogation

It's important to learn to ask questions in a way that causes new thought or reflection rather than defense or survival brain thinking. As a Practical Application of the Operating Principles, learn to ask questions of yourself, of another person, and of groups in a way that shines a light on current conditions and the gaps to close in order to experience real accomplishment. Here are some sample questions listed under a couple of scenarios to get you started. Notice which questions are repeated and add these to your generic question library!

While you are practicing asking questions keep these Operating Principles in mind:

Principle #1: Be Present, Stay in the Game

Principle #2: Listen Newly, Be Intentionally Slow to Understand

Principle #3: Take Myself Lightly

Principle #4: Declare There Is Nothing Wrong or Broken *Here and Now*

Principle #5: Explore *truths*: Mine, Theirs, and Ours

Questions to Explore Reality

Example Situation: A Project is "Off-Track"

<u>Exploring *my truths*, ask and answer these questions for yourself:</u>

- What do I know? What don't I know?

- What would I like to learn more about or understand on a deeper level?

- What is my understanding of my role in the project to date?

- What do I see as my role moving forward?

- How critical is this issue on a scale of 1–10 in terms of importance? In terms of urgency?

- What are the consequences that I see? Opportunities?

- Where am I stuck in "It's just wrong"?

- What interpretations, conclusions, judgments, or decisions have I already made that might preclude me from being an effective contributor in collaborating for resolution?

- What will it cost me to give those up, listen newly, and "explore truths"?

- What is possible if I do?

- Am I willing to have the ultimate goal be more important than my preconceived conclusions, interpretations, decisions, and judgments?

Exploring *their truths,* ask these questions of another person:

- What are the issues from their perspective?

- How did the project get to this place?

- What has their understanding of their role been?

- How critical is this issue to them on a scale of 1–10 in terms of importance? In terms of urgency?

- What are the consequences that they see? Opportunities?

- What data points can they share about from their vantage point?

- How did they arrive at their conclusions, what is the background?

- What has changed, if anything?

- What can they offer as possible pathways or solutions?

- What are the most important considerations moving forward?

- What is missing for success – from their viewpoint?

- What do they see as their role moving forward?

- What other resources are required?

Exploring *our truths,* ask these questions to a group:

- What do we know? What don't we know?

- What *was* the ultimate goal of the project? Is that still valid?

- What is the current status of the project with respect to timetable, budget, and resources?

- What are the current internal/external conditions we are facing?

- Who is impacted by a change in status or progress?

- What are the consequences to the organization, client, or internal team if it remains on the current track?

- What ideas can be generated for how to close the gap between the original intention and the current projection? Who could help with that?

- What resources would be required to get the project back on track?

- What is currently missing? If we had that—could it work? What else?

- What other information would be useful for our decision-making?

- Who else could contribute to our understanding of the issues?

- Who else could contribute to our solution/option set?

- What questions are we avoiding?

- How do we define the gap between the current status and our goal (Yonder Star)?

Example Situation:
Considering Aspects of Making a Big Decision

Exploring *my truths*, ask and answer these questions for yourself:

- What is the purpose and what are the intended outcomes of this decision?

- How critical is this decision on a scale of 1–10 in terms of importance? In terms of urgency?

- What are the consequences of a stalled decision or a "no decision" decision?

- What is at risk? For me? For others? For the organization? For customers? The community?

- A year from now how will I be measuring success?

- What do I know? What do I know that I don't know?

- What would I like to learn more about or understand on a deeper level?

- Who could help me understand what I know I don't know?

- Who could illuminate what I don't know that I don't know?

- Is this one I must make, or can it be delegated as a growth opportunity?

- What roles could others take in assuring the best possible decision is made?

- What interpretations, conclusions, judgments, or decisions have I already made that might preclude me from being an effective decision maker?

Exploring *their truths,* ask these questions of another person:

Note: If you will be making the final decision, be sure to let the other person(s) know your decision making process so that they realize they are contributing to a decision that you will ultimately be making based on the information and perspectives you have gathered. Also, don't ask these questions if you have already made your decision!

- What are the issues to consider regarding this pending decision from their perspective?

- What role do they see or what contribution can they make toward making a good decision?

- What are the consequences that they see? Opportunities?

- What data points can they share about from their vantage point that might help close the gaps in your understanding?

- How did they arrive at their conclusions; what is the background?

- What can they offer as possible pathways or solutions?

- What are the areas of consideration that you may not yet see that they can illuminate (what you don't even know that you don't know)?

- What are the most important considerations moving forward?

Exploring *our truths,* ask these questions to a group:

- What is the purpose and what are the intended outcomes of this decision? Or you might share the purpose and intended outcomes with the group before asking the balance of the questions.

- How critical is this decision on a scale of 1–10 in terms of importance? In terms of urgency? This is more information that you might be sharing with the group before asking the following questions depending on the situation— rather than making it a guessing game!

- What are the consequences of a stalled decision or a "no decision" decision?

- What is at risk? For our team? For the organization? For customers? The community?

- A year from now how will we be measuring success?

- What do we already know? What do we know that we don't know?

- What would we like to learn more about or understand on a deeper level?

- Who could help us understand what we know we don't know?

- Who could help us understand what we don't even know that we don't know?

- What outside expertise could help us?

Eliminate the Buts!

The word "but" can wreak havoc in conversations. It is an unconscious speaking habit that can narrow your own pathway of thinking, highlight contradiction versus coexisting perspectives, create defensiveness, and discount the value of appreciative comments.

Shift from limited either/or thinking by using a simple (not easy) technique of using "and" rather than "but." This shift in language signals your mind that two seemingly disparate ideas can in fact coexist. This structure puts the mind into curiosity and creative problem-solving mode; going to work on how to reach the Yonder Star with the coexistence of two (or more) differing realities. Using the word "but" between the two thoughts signals that the second half of the statement contradicts the first half. Your mind has to then resolve which one is right or which one wins—a much narrower and less productive path.

If another person said the following to you, after you shared your perspective with them, what would your instant reaction be? "I appreciate your perspective on this issue, *but* I have a different point of view." What retort sprang up? "But" used in this way simply means "disregard all that has gone before." The focus is on the second, *valid,* half of the sentence. Now you are into the defense of your perspective and have lost sight of the purpose of the discussion in the first place! What if the other person said this to you instead: "I appreciate your perspective on this issue, *and* I have a different point of view." What question pops up now? This and other language shifts only work if your underlying intention is to cause a more productive interaction with the way you speak and listen.

Here are more examples to demonstrate the effect on willingness to collaborate and make changes. Notice in this next example how it evokes a mood shift from despair to possibility. "Our goal is 15% revenue growth this year, *but* the economy is really hurting us." Can you hear your brain going to despair and victimhood? There is nothing we can do to change the economy, after all! Instead: "Our goal is 15% revenue growth *and* the economy has been hurting us." Did you recognize a mental shift to considering what, given a tough economy, you might be able to do now?

What happens in this example? "We met the attendance criteria *but* we missed on the income projections." Said this way, the second half of the statement invalidates the first. Shift to: "We met the attendance criteria *and* missed the income projections." This statement has the two data points sitting side by side, coexisting. Another example: "I like the way you took charge of the event and demonstrated leadership *but* next time there *should* be more time between the speakers."

If you aspire to really mastering this material, replace "should" with "could" as well as replacing "but" with "and"! For example, "I like the way you took charge of the event and demonstrated leadership, *and* next time there *could* be more time between the speakers." By substituting "and" for "but," you allow both perceptions to be valid and be held concurrently. By using "could" instead of "should," you take the right/wrong positioning out of the statement and simply offer your viewpoint as something to be considered.

When these words demonstrate that you have truly shifted your frame of reference and are approaching your interactions guided by the Operating Principles, it works. Otherwise, no matter how you change what you say, other people still hear your "ands," "buts," and "shoulds" anyway! Remarkably, your true feelings and perspectives speak louder than your words.

Unmasking the Issue—Reframing "Wrong"

A key leadership skill is the ability to reframe issues, opportunities and situations so that the most creative and productive forward movement can take place. One of the major issue-masking and survival-brain-generated habits of mind gets started with the label "wrong." You have to be able to constructively reframe *for yourself* when you are dwelling on the lower line of the Leadership Choice Point or in the Distress-Upset Emotional Zone. The mental framework generated by "wrong" creates a very strong pull in that direction for you and for others.

Review the chart on the next page and consider which of these comments on the left-hand side of the column might be typical for you. Check the reframing option on the right-hand side to see how it might shift your thinking, creativity and the direction of the conversation. Practice reframing often when presented with low stakes situations to build your muscle with this skill so that you will have it readily available to do the heavy lifting when you are facing a significant challenge.

Practice Operating Principle #4: *Declare There Is Nothing Wrong or Broken Here and Now* as you read through the examples. What is your internal dialogue? Is it critical or curious? Are you telling yourself "These will never work!"; "That's not me!"; "That sounds wimpy!" Or are you asking yourself "What if?"; "What might be possible here?"; "How could I incorporate some of these to help me practice my skills at reframing in general?" To fully experience the difference as you read through the examples, imagine someone saying these thing to you—perhaps an authority figure, your boss, a board member, etc. What is your instant and automatic reaction? Where do you think the conversation would go from there?

Then consider the reframed comment on the right-hand side. What if that person had said it that way? What is different about your own reaction? Where could the conversation go from there? Finally, what reaction do you want from others when you speak?

While you are reading through the examples, keep these Operating Principles in mind:

Principle #1: Be Present, Stay in the Game

Principle #2: Listen Newly, Be Intentionally Slow to Understand

Principle #4: Declare There Is Nothing Wrong or Broken *Here and Now*

Principle #8: Confront and Deal with Real Issues

Examples: Reframe for More Accuracy & Collaboration Opportunities

Focusing on "Wrong", judging, attacking/defending	Reframe to own my perception, exploring *truths* and being responsible for what gets heard.
"I disagree…"	"My perspective is very different, would you share with me how you came to your point of view on this?
"That's wrong."	"That has not been my experience."
"You're wrong."	"Help me understand your perspective — I'm not there yet."
"This part is wrong."	"This part is out of spec on the overall length. The spec says ____ and the length of this part is ____."
"This report is wrong"	"The totals on this page do not balance with the totals on the back page."
"This report is useless."	"In order to use this report to make decisions, the data will have to be translated into a more summary informational format. I suggest…"
"The process is wrong."	"How has the process contributed to the outcome we are currently experiencing? There may be ways to streamline and improve it to improve results."
"That's not what he said to do."	"I heard the instructions differently."
"We have the wrong people assigned."	"Have we really done a good job of matching people's skills to job requirements?"
"Our meetings are always a waste of time"	"I have some suggestions for how to improve the value of our weekly meetings."

Finding Alignment— Moving the Conversation and the Focus "One Up"

Many teams persist in conversations of disagreement or conflicting agendas, wasting energy and time and risking deterioration of relationships, respect, and future capacity for collaboration. The most effective people recognize this stalled or deteriorating state as quickly as possible in conversation, stop driving their own agenda, and proactively move the conversation up to a higher level of alignment before continuing to discuss the current topic.

The Vision-Focused Leadership diagram first introduced in the Essential Notions—Section One and again in this Practical Application shows how you can use the concept of moving the conversation 'one up' to reach a new level of alignment, reuniting the participants in a cohesive team of collaborators rather than a competitive group of debaters.

In competitions and debates there is always someone or something to attack, defeat, or diminish. In unproductive group interactions, the competitive or debating nature moves from outside competitors and obstacles to things like considering your own teammates as competitors for airtime or for who has the best and brightest idea. In addition, inordinate amounts of time are spent on discussing issues that are irrelevant or sidetracking from the real issue at hand. Practice using this Practical Application in a number of everyday conversations so that you will have built an experience base and new capacities by the next time a really intense conversation requires its application!

Vision-Focused Leadership

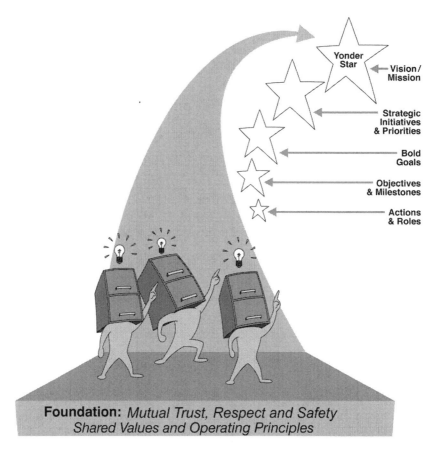

Foundation: *Mutual Trust, Respect and Safety*
Shared Values and Operating Principles

This hierarchy of Yonder Stars works because actions are designed to serve objectives and goals, goals to serve strategic initiatives, and strategies to serve mission and vision; not the other direction. So when you are stuck in a conversation, it makes sense to reach up and tether the conversation to a higher order of priority to get a better view.

If there is no alignment at this next Yonder Star level of the goal, or if the topics you are discussing *are* goals and objectives and the conversation stalls or deteriorates, move the conversation up another level to the next Yonder Star of strategy. Continue the process of looking for a higher place where you are all connected until you can reconnect with each other and return to Productive Dialogue. That new level is the level where you can interact as team members with a clear intention and direction for the conversation rather than as adversaries.

The Operating Principles to review for this application are:

Principle #4: Declare There Is Nothing Wrong or Broken *Here and Now*

Principle #5: Explore *truths*: Mine, Theirs, and Ours

Principle #6: Confront and Deal with Real Issues

Principle #8: Make It Safe *and* Productive

Work through the following outline for reaching "one-up" in your interactions to achieve alignment.

Outline: Finding Alignment
Moving the Conversation and the Focus "One Up"

When you first notice that the topic or issue is stalled or progress is deteriorating:

1. Stop pushing your own agenda—listen and determine what level of focus is taking place—action conversation, goals conversation, strategy conversation?

2. Intervene in the direction of the conversation by asking a question about the Yonder Star that is one level up from the current focus. Use your own words to check in and see if there is alignment amongst the group about that higher level. For example, if the conversation is stalled regarding choosing a method or pathway (an action item) move the conversation back up to the goal level:

   > "Hang on, could I just check something out here? The reason we are even discussing these various methods is because of our mutual goal of XX. Is that right? Aren't we all here because we are committed to accomplishing XX and have run into some tough road blocks?"

3. Restate the goal (Yonder Star) of *this* conversation. Example:

   > "OK...so the goal of this conversation is to brainstorm and ultimately determine the most effective pathway forward that best utilizes our existing resources. Is that our mutual criteria?"

4. Engage in inquiry, explore and connect. Examples:

   - "Help me understand how this (topic) connects to our overall goal of XX."

- "Help me understand how this (action) you are recommending helps us get closer to our goal of XX."

- "Help me understand how solving the problem of YY will help us get closer to our goal of XX."

- "Is this the most leveraged action we can take to move toward our goal of XX?"

Practical Application #6:

Productive Delegation— Building Confidence and Accountability

One of the most common complaints we hear from our executive clients is that their people are not "accountable" or that they have a hard time holding other people accountable for their assigned projects. Failure to delegate clearly and effectively at the start can often lead to a requirement for much tougher conversations down the road. Since many people avoid difficult conversations, the best way to minimize them is to set things up for success at the beginning. Delegating productively requires practicing a number of the Essential Notions, including Self-Generated Accountability, defining a Yonder Star, owning your perceptions, using "I" statements, and being direct and sensitive, as well as the following Operating Principles:

> Principle #5: Explore *truths*: Mine, Theirs, and Ours

> Principle #7: Be Responsible for Creating Value

> Principle #8: Make It Safe *and* Productive

To help you apply the Operating Principles to a delegation situation we have provided an outline to walk you through a productive delegation process, a preparation worksheet and some steps suggesting what to do if the project gets off course after the delegation. Be sure to read the Practical Application: *Project Performance Review—Achieving Clarity and Alignment* later in this section. You may also need to use your newly formed muscle from the Practical Application: *Questions to Explore Reality—Curiosity versus Interrogation* from the example *A Project is Off-Track* earlier in this section.

Outline: Productive Delegation
Building Confidence and Accountability

In the Beginning

Before you meet about the project for the first time, ask and answer these seven questions for yourself:

1. What is the *ideal outcome* (Yonder Star) of this project, how will success be measured (quantitatively and time bound), and what internal and external resources are available?

2. What is the *key reason* or motivation for delegation? For example:

   ▪ The other projects/priorities on my plate are more strategic, higher leverage, or require my unique contribution. (Note how this is different than "Because…I don't have time for this!")

   ▪ Another team member can best contribute the skills required.

   ▪ It is a developmental opportunity.

3. What are the *opportunities* generated by successful completion?

4. What are the *consequences* of project failure or missed timing?

5. What are the main reasons for *choosing the specific person* to whom you intend to assign this project?

6. What are the *resources* that will be *required* to successfully complete the project in the timeframe envisioned?

7. Force rank for yourself the criteria of quality, timing and cost/investment. No, they can't all be equally important. When push comes to shove, which criteria rules?

   - *Quality*—Is it quality, no matter what it costs or how long it takes;

   - *Deadline*—Or, if it isn't done by X date, it won't matter how good it is;

   - *Budget*—Or, If it costs more than $X, it doesn't matter how fast or how good it is?

At the First Meeting

1. *Discuss* the seven points listed above.

2. Ask for the other person's perspective and ask what *clarifying* questions he or she has at this point.

3. Check in to see how this assignment may *impact* his or her *other assignments* and due dates and align on adjustments as necessary. If necessary, schedule times with other people who are impacted by any scheduling or resource adjustments.

4. Set up *"check-in"* points and a process (depending on project duration, scope, opportunity, and risks). Set and calendar a specific date, time, and place for the first check-in or project review. Ask the other person to come prepared with the information or measurements you have discussed as well as an agenda for what help, resources, coaching, and advice he or she might need from you. Re-emphasize the force ranked criteria of quality, timing, and cost/investment. Encourage the person to save questions and discussion items for the check-in meetings, if appropriate. If the person doesn't think it can wait until a scheduled meeting, then encourage meeting sooner.

Don't discourage communication; however, having a definite, scheduled check-in date will help you both manage your time more effectively.

5. Have a *conversation about your conversations* (see earlier application) especially covering how you will connect and interact if the project gets off course regarding time, quality, budget, or resources.

At the First Check-In Meeting

1. *Have the meeting!* Keep the date and time you set aside. If change is unavoidable, reschedule the follow-up meeting as close to the original date as possible. Notify the other party as far in advance as possible of the need to reschedule.

2. Have the *other person start the meeting*, move through the update material, and ask questions. Let them know that this is, most importantly, *their scheduled time* to use you as a resource for the project. If you have any unanswered questions, ask them at the end. Peppering people with questions that they may answer in their update trains them to wait for you to ask questions rather than be proactive with sharing the information you have agreed is important to have at the update meetings. It also takes away ownership!

3. *Clarify and align* on any new decisions, direction, or resources, if applicable, resulting from the project review session. Communicate to your own peers and boss if there are changes that impact them.

4. *Have a brief conversation* about this conversation. Ask:

    a. "What really worked about this session from your perspective?" Wait to get feedback. "Here's what worked from my perspective..."

b. "What would make it (even) more productive for next time from your perspective?" Wait to get feedback. "Here's what would make it more productive next time from my perspective…"

Be sure to use "I" statements when answering these for yourself and separate the person from the issue. For example:

- Rather than "It really worked that you showed up on time," try "It worked well for me that we were able to start right on time."

- Rather than "It would make it more productive if you were more prepared!" try "It would be more productive for me if we reviewed the XYZ Report during our review sessions."

- Rather than "It would be more productive if you weren't so defensive and full of excuses!" try "It would be more productive for me to fully understand the hard data and its implications for the project's success first, and then have you layer in your feelings and concerns about it."

Set the next date(s) and time(s)

At the End of the Project

1. Have a *completion meeting* to review, celebrate and learn.

2. *Review the outcomes* in light of the shared Yonder Star.

3. *Celebrate* all accomplishments in the project itself, your partnering in the delegation process, and learning that took place

(see the Practical Application: *Acknowledgment, Appreciation, Celebration and Completion* later in this section).

4. Have a conversation about *what was learned* during the process that can be applied moving forward—about projects in general, about your working relationship, etc.

5. *Declare it complete!*

Course Correction: When the Assignment Gets "Off Course"

What if, from your perspective, the project gets "off course"?

This could even include that you realize you have no idea whether it is on course or not. Bring it up in the next project review meeting if one is imminent or, if appropriate, call for an interim course correction meeting.

Do not wait for the project to fail! Share what you have learned or what you are seeing or not seeing that has you believe that the project is "off course." Be sure to check out the Practical Application: *Project Performance Review—Achieving Clarity and Alignment* later in this section.

1. *Share the "warning signals"* you have observed that have had you intervene and call this meeting—as an opportunity for a developmental conversation rather than an opportunity for make-wrong or blame.

2. *Validate your perspective* with real-time information (reality check).

3. Ask *what is missing* that could be put in place to get back on track or what roadblock is in the way that could be removed.

4. *Brainstorm solutions*. Ask what additional resources or support may be required.

5. *Align* on new pathways or actions.

6. Return to *regularly scheduled* review meetings or schedule an interim follow-up meeting, depending on the nature of the "warning signals."

Productive Delegation Preparation Form

Project/Assignment Name: _____

1. **Project Description** _____
   Ideal Outcome(s): _____
   Quantitative Measurement(s): _____
   Resources/Budget Allocated: _____

2. **Key Reason(s) for Delegation:** _____

3. **New Opportunities Possible** _____
   For Company/Department: _____
   For Client/Client Department: _____
   For Me/My Development: _____
   For Person Assigned/His or Her Development: _____

4. **Consequences of Failure** _____
   For Company/Department: _____
   For Client/Client Department: _____
   For Me/My Development: _____
   For Person Assigned/His or Her Development: _____

5. **Person Assigned:** _____
   Key Reason for choosing the person for assignment: _____

6. **Key Resources required:** _____

7. **Force Ranked Criteria:** ___Quality ___Deadline ___ Budget ___ Resources

(This means there can only be one characteristic that is #1, #2 and so forth. Choose!)

First Meeting Scheduled:

Date: _____ **Time:** _____ **Location:**

Productive Meetings— Increasing Engagement and Outcomes

atrick Lencione's book, *Death by Meetings,* has been a big seller. Clearly, the amount and value of the time people spend in meetings and the effectiveness or lack thereof is top of mind for many. In addition, the time drain of heavy meeting schedules has a huge influence on a team's productivity.

Reflecting on your recent experience in meetings, what has your role been in any meeting that you called or in which you were a participant? Have you been an unwitting victim to an unproductive event or did you generate a productive environment? Did you contribute to identifying and dealing with real issues, building on the comments of others and recommending structures for accomplishment? Did you prepare a draft Purpose and Intended Outcomes document for distribution and discussion? What part of your meeting's value are you ready to own now?

As you respond to these questions, draw on these Operating Principles:

Principle #5: Explore *truths*: Mine, Theirs, and Ours

Principle #6: Confront and Deal with Real Issues

Principle #7: Be Responsible for Creating Value

Principle #9: Be Responsible for What Gets Heard

When you are preparing for a meeting, ask yourself the questions on the next two pages and then use the instructions that follow to develop a draft Purpose and Intended Outcomes. When you have the meeting, be ready to add value through intentional actions designed with these Operating Principles in mind.

Productive Meeting Recommendations

If You Called the Meeting

- ✓ Have you included all the constituents (regardless of titles) who have a stake in what is to be discussed or decided?
- ✓ Have you included people only because of titles? Who are you afraid to leave out? Ask what's at risk if you leave them out?
- ✓ Have you created a draft purpose and intended outcomes for the meeting which then guides your agenda and time allocations?
- ✓ Have you identified how the intended outcomes relate to the Yonder Star?
- ✓ Do you start and end your meetings on time?
- ✓ Do you start your meeting by gaining group alignment regarding the outcomes?
- ✓ During the meeting, does the group observe the Operating Principles?
- ✓ Are you soliciting participation from each participant, especially the ones who tend to be more quiet or introspective?
- ✓ Do you summarize what was accomplished during the meeting and the next steps, as well as clarify who, what, and by when?
- ✓ Do you keep a "Parking Lot" list of important yet off-agenda items that arise during the meeting?
- ✓ Do you set a "next time," if appropriate, to review progress and work through any new issues or "Parking Lot" topics?
- ✓ Do you save time at the end of the meeting to openly survey the participants about what worked in this meeting? Do you preserve that learning as process for next time and explore how the next meeting could be even more productive?
- ✓ Do you check in with participants between meetings, especially if they report to you?

Productive Meeting Recommendations

As a Participant

- ✓ Do you check for the purpose and intended outcomes of the meeting and form expectations for your own participation?
- ✓ Do you consider the value to you and others of your participation and get clear about what you are to provide to or get from the meeting?
- ✓ If you are presenting have you developed and communicated the purpose and intended outcomes of your own section?
- ✓ Have you asked to be uninvited if neither you nor the person who called the meeting can state the value your participation would bring?
- ✓ Have you reviewed the list of participants with respect to the purpose and intended outcomes and suggested other participants who have a similar or even greater stake in the outcomes?
- ✓ In the meeting, are you attentive, with your BlackBerry or PDA turned off?
- ✓ Are you judging what each person says or are you considering points of view with open curiosity?
- ✓ Are you competing or interrupting to get in your brilliant perspective, or are you building on the ideas of others to create deeper exploration?
- ✓ Are you being defensive of yourself or others, or are you putting that aside to be able to listen for and share what really happened?
- ✓ Are you connecting the issues or opportunities to the Yonder Star?
- ✓ Are you listening for how you can forward the conversation?
- ✓ Have you brought your problem-solving mind-set?

Productive Meetings: Developing Purpose and Intended Outcomes

The process of developing Purpose and Intended Outcomes is valuable for many situations. In our work with clients we use this process for every client engagement from multi-day facilitations to an executive coaching assignment. In this practical application we are specifically addressing how to use this process regarding meetings. As you read through the description and review the form, think of where else you could use this process beneficially—perhaps wherever you are working toward alignment or clarity!

Productive Meetings – Purpose and Intended Outcomes

Always label your Purpose and Intended Outcomes document as a *DRAFT*, until presented, discussed and each participant has had an opportunity for alignment. Reviewing and gaining alignment at the beginning of a meeting is the first opportunity to generate group alignment—get everyone on the same page. Consider that one of the intended outcomes of preparing this document is to generate a *context* of alignment where *content* can be dealt with productively. Until you can align on "Why are we here and what are we to accomplish?" how can you expect to gain alignment on anything during the meeting itself? Once everyone Is on the same page, it will be much easier during the meeting to steer the discussion back on course and to use a "Parking Lot" list to track important—yet off agenda items—deserving of further discussion at another appointed time. Invest the time up front to develop the document, it helps clarify your own thinking. Invest the time at the beginning of the meeting to review, adjust and align. Be patient, over time it will get much easier to prepare and to facilitate the process. The increased productivity and collaboration will be well worth it.

Guidelines: Developing Purpose and Intended Outcomes

Purpose Statements

- A purpose statement is clear, concise and compelling and answers the question—why do this? What difference will it make?

- A purpose statement creates context. It is powerfully articulated in a way that points to the future—or more accurately—pulls for the future. What is the Yonder Star that this meeting or interaction is intended to move forward? What is the bigger picture?

- The purpose statement allows others to stand with us in alignment—it's a tool for mobilizing ownership, participation, a shared commitment and a shared vision.

Intended Outcomes

- Intended outcomes are specific and distinct. If you stand in the future—at the completion of the activity—and look back, this is the list of what was accomplished.

- To create a list of intended outcomes, look from many angles: What will be accomplished for us? For others? What will be learned? What new organizational capabilities will be developed? What new openings for action will be revealed?

- Have the list be complete, inclusive, clear, and unambiguous.

- State them as having been completed.

- Order the list in a way that communicates clearly—that rolls out naturally in the direction of achieving the purpose. For a meeting, a well-organized list of intended outcomes can become the agenda.

Worksheet: Purpose and Intended Outcomes

Purpose: (What's the point? What is the bigger picture or Yonder Star for having the meeting anyway?)

To create the possibility for _____

_____

_____

Intended Outcomes:

1. To have

   _____

   _____

2. To have

   _____

   _____

3. To have

   _____

   _____

4. To have

   _____

   _____

5. To have

   _____

   _____

6. To have taken ourselves lightly!

Project Performance Review— Achieving Clarity and Alignment

At times you may be confronted with the situation where you see that an otherwise qualified team member is failing to perform on a particular project or area of their responsibility and yet he or she does not see it the way you do, or at least will not admit it.

One temptation is to hint around, not wanting to "upset the apple cart" or face the risk of getting embroiled in a difficult and time-consuming conversation. Your action may include indirect references, less-than-straightforward statements, sarcasm, and disguised requests like "we really need to get this work done."

While all of the Operating Principles are essential to engaging in this type of conversation with grace and ease, here are a few key principles to review:

> Principle #2: Listen Newly, Be Intentionally Slow To Understand
>
> Principle #4: Declare There is Nothing Wrong or Broken *Here and Now*
>
> Principle #5: Explore *truths*: Mine, Theirs, and Ours
>
> Principle #6: Confront and Deal With Real Issues
>
> Principle #9: Be Responsible for What Gets Heard

The model to keep in mind while engaged in this dialogue is the Productive Dialogue Zone.

Productive Dialogue Zone

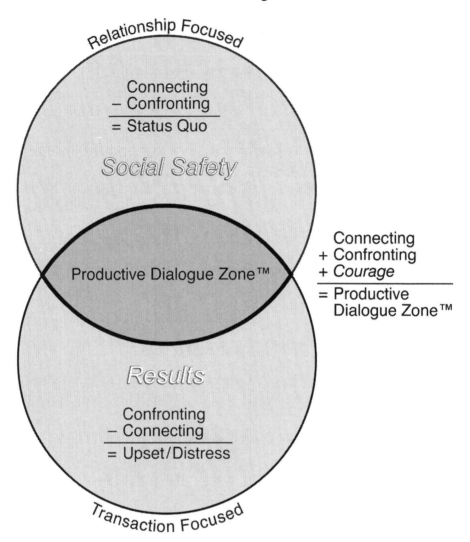

There are several direct *and* sensitive steps you can take in addressing progress and getting corrective action while maintaining the relationship and being efficient with both parties' time. Use the seven steps in the outline we have provided to have a productive project performance review.

Outline: Project Performance Review
Achieving Clarity and Alignment

1. *Schedule a progress review* at a specific time and location that works for both of you and where you will not be interrupted.

2. Be sure you both have allowed enough time to *stay with the conversation* until it is complete.

3. *State your view of the job expectations* and see if they are clear and mutually understood.

   a. If they aren't, then at least you have identified the issue. Go over the specifics again and request a commitment to the agreed-upon work and due date or a new date if the original date is no longer feasible.

   b. If you both agree on the work and due dates and disagree on progress, then your job is to explore for mutually observable performance data; tasks, quality standards, and due dates. Check to see that you have the best data, are assessing progress from the same standpoint, and are not acting out of emotion. Bottom line, it is essential to mutually sort out the way that it is and the way it isn't before you can have any really successful conversations for altering performance and producing the desired outcomes.

   c. Your job is to shift the focus of the conversation "up and out" from confronting each other to mutually confronting expected results, due dates, the actual rate of progress, and what will be required to get the job done.

4. Once you both agree on the status of the work and the short-fall, *ask, "What happened?"* Listen newly and openly, and keep asking until the other person has been able to fully say what he or she has to say. You don't have to agree, just listen.

5. Mutually *set new targets* or agree on additional resources to be brought to bear to assure originally scheduled completion.

6. Set up any *new tracking or reporting* you both agree is needed to be confident going forward.

7. Ask what the team member has *learned*.

Dialogue for Making a Role Change or Closing a Performance Gap

Almost every client we have comes up against situations where someone is not performing satisfactorily or the job the person has been doing is going to change significantly. In either case, our clients often struggle with identifying and working in the "Productive Dialogue Zone." The client starts a conversation with the person and fails to follow through with the uncomfortable part. Nothing changes, of course. The client then gets emotional, starts issuing directives, the person's attitude plunges, and no real change is created.

Productive Dialogue Zone

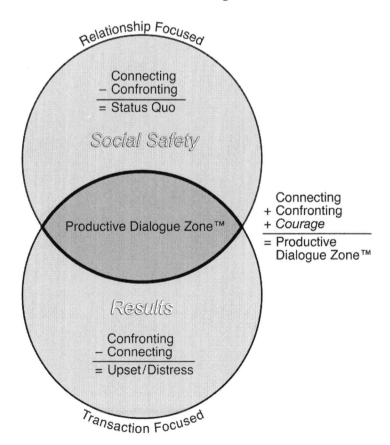

Referring to the model, you will remember that your first task is to be connected with the person so you can confront the issue together. "Not so easy," you say. "The minute I bring up the situation, he or she gets upset and we get nowhere." It's common for a person called into a performance conversation to immediately hear criticism and for the person bringing up the question to be hesitant or tentative, such that one or both go on the defensive. Being connected is a fundamental requirement for a Productive Dialogue, and yet this seems nearly impossible to accomplish when the subject is extremely uncomfortable for one or more parties.

While all of the Operating Principles are essential to engaging in this type of conversation with grace and ease, here are a few to particularly keep in mind:

> Principle #1: Be Present, Stay in the Game

> Principle #4: Declare There is Nothing Wrong or Broken *Here and Now*

> Principle #8: Make It Safe *and* Productive

> Principle #9: Be Responsible for What Gets Heard

We have designed the following "recipe" for the conversation to increase your odds of success. Our approach is based on the view that you cannot get anyone to really change beliefs and behaviors simply by telling him or her to do so—only the person can change him or herself. You may get vicious compliance by forcing your will without real, productive change that then calls forth the best from the person. To that, we add David Whyte's assertion that "no one needs to change but everyone has to have the conversation." If you can't make people change and yet they have to have the conversation, how do you engage with them in a way that causes real results? The essential ingredient is choice. Have a conversation that brings people to choice—their own choice. Use the following "recipe" exactly as written until you get your balance. After you have had some successes, add your own unique spices.

274

Recipe: Dialogue for Making a Role Change or Closing a Performance Gap

Before the Conversation:

Clarify your intention and write down your Yonder Star for the conversation. To have it empower the two of you, it will contain a statement that addresses, at a minimum:

- ✓ honoring the person involved (who he or she is);
- ✓ the specific physical and financial results to be achieved;
- ✓ your commitment regarding the type of relationship you intend to have after the conversation is over.

Set up a specific time and place where you can have an undisturbed conversation until completion, including time to work through any upset, if necessary.

Opening Statement:

1. Start by letting the person know that you are going to have a rigorous conversation (topic of performance gap or job/role change) with them where you will describe what is required and ask them to make some choices.

2. Describe the new job to be done or review the specific, measurable performance and behaviors required to successfully perform the job the person currently has (at which he or she is failing—the performance gap).

3. Let the person know that he or she does not have to change, does not even have to do that job. From now on, however, the person that is doing that job will perform it as you have described. You are creating a fork in the road and asking the person to choose—perform the new way or engage in a

conversation for some other job, either within the company or somewhere else.

Example Opening Statements:

- "John, my intention in this meeting is to have a rigorous conversation about the role you currently have in the organization and the outcomes that role is expected to produce (or will be changing to)."

- "The issue I'm here to discuss today is the gap between the expected outcomes in your department of X and the actual outcomes of Y, or the impact your leadership and communication style have on the culture of your work team, etc. These results are required for successful performance in the role of _____."

- "You aren't required to change or to do that job, however, from now on the person that is doing that job will perform it as I have described."

- "I'd like to get your feedback to determine if *you* are willing to make the changes and corrections required for that job."

After Their Comments or Questions, If Any:

1. To make it a clear choice, be straight about the fact that you do not know whether there is another job in the firm that fits and meets the person's pay desires. You will be fair about giving the person a shot if there is such a job or working with them on outplacement if not.

2. If the person says he or she will commit to do the existing job successfully or will take on the new role, as described,

emphasize the elements of the role that are currently missing in the person's performance and behaviors and suggest that it is not a good fit unless significant changes occur. You may ask the person to go home and think about it overnight or over the weekend.

3. If the person still says he or she will do the job and perform it well, it is time for an even more rigorous conversation in which you point out that, based on past performance; the person isn't on good ground to make such a promise. You will agree to give the person a shot and be fully supportive with added training, mentoring, coaching, etc. The person will, however, have to find such a program, acceptable to you, and take on his or her own growth and development.

4. If the person decides not to step up, then it's time for another level of choice. Do you have another job in the firm that the person can do and, if so, is it at the same pay grade? If not, be rigorous about the new arrangement and bring the person to choice again.

5. Rather than let the person take on a new job to which he or she is really not committed, work together on an outplacement plan that allows the person to maintain dignity and also survive financially.

A Few Caveats to Keep in Mind:

✓ Remember that your own discomfort about being direct can easily get in the way. That's all about you and the remedy will come from your chair. Keep noticing and clearing your own feelings.

✓ Remember that you are dealing with someone who is probably experiencing threat or criticism or both. Your job is to focus the confronting conversation on the qualities that will be exhibited by the person who will be doing the existing or new job (Yonder Star). Emphasize that he or she does not have to have those qualities to be a valuable person, only to have that job.

✓ We are reminded of the scenario used by the child psychologist who has her patient "talk to the puppet" on her hand rather than talk to her, an adult authority figure. In your case, the puppet is the Yonder Star (job expectations performed well) that the two of you are confronting together. Focusing on that, you will be much more able to address the gaps that you feel would have to be filled if the person were to take on the job.

✓ You may well have a series of conversations to get to your intended outcomes. There is no requirement to get it all done in one or two. "Rome wasn't built in a day," Mom used to say.

Acknowledgement, Appreciation, Celebration and Completion

Some of our clients struggle with acknowledgement, showing appreciation, and celebrating results with the team. Some of the common threads we hear behind the issue are:

- Our clients are high performers themselves and are always focusing on the next thing, so they have already moved on by the time the accomplishment is complete.

- By the time the scorecard is done (contract has been awarded, work completed, numbers tallied, etc.) it seems anticlimactic.

- Various key team members are traveling, and by the time a date can be found that all can be present, it seems irrelevant.

- Some of our clients are the "glass-is-half-empty" types and focus on the parts that were not achieved or where they think the team could have done better. Nothing is ever enough for them so celebrating would reward less than excellent work.

- Fear that acknowledging someone will give that person a big head or the person will want more money or both.

Acknowledgement and celebration are essential to fueling passion, making people feel valid and valuable, and giving the team a real sense of progress that makes it all worthwhile. People who do not get a chance to celebrate a new level of accomplishment often fall back to an old, lower level where they just repeat what they know how to do rather than reaching for yet another higher aspiration. Acknowledging and celebrating accomplishments helps lock in a "new normal." Most high performers are aware that if they produce extraordinary results, they will be asked for even more next time. To support them in going for it, it works to show full appreciation for the current results. If they don't get a chance to celebrate and complete the accomplishment, the lingering incompletion may act as a "suppress button," perhaps for years, and may limit both their effectiveness and willingness to set and go for challenging goals the next time.

The model to keep in mind while engaged in this dialogue is the Leadership Choice Point. The stretch, risk and uncertainty of operating on the upper line of the Leadership Choice Point to accomplish higher aspirational goals generates endorphins, and other biochemistry that exhilarate and support success. You want to affirm and lock in how it feels to accomplish and win. Those are the "good stress" results of Vision-Focused Leadership.

Leadership Choice Point

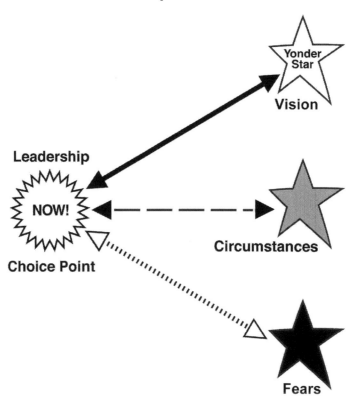

While all of the Operating Principles are helpful to engaging in these types of conversations with grace and ease, here are a few to especially keep in mind:

Principle #2: Listen Newly, Be Intentionally Slow To Understand

Principle #3: Take Myself Lightly

Principle #5: Explore *truths*: Mine, Theirs, and Ours

Principle #8: Make It Safe *and* Productive

If you find yourself among the holdouts when it comes to celebration, here's a checklist for you:

Checklist for Hold-outs!

- ✓ *Identify* the unconscious and unexamined story or interpretation from your own life that is running your behavior.
- ✓ *Take responsibility* for your own bias and juxtapose that with the gains for the team if they get to "put a marker down" on the accomplishment and anchor it with a fun time together.
- ✓ Let the participants know how much you *appreciate* their performance and their contribution to fulfilling the Yonder Star.
- ✓ Ask what the team members would see as an appropriate celebration for the accomplishment and do your best to put that together. When you get good at this, set it up in advance so it adds to the incentive in the first place.
- ✓ *Celebrate* as soon and as often as possible, perhaps at each key milestone, so that it becomes a habit for the group. Participate yourself. Your presence is essential, as it demonstrates your commitment and appreciation much more than your words.

If the Project Hasn't Been Fully Completed

A special word has to be said about *completion*. What we mean here is the notion that something has run its full course. Even if only part of a goal was achieved, or perhaps even more importantly when the team fell short, it is very productive to complete the intention by doing the following:

1. Get together with the individual or team involved and *confront the results together.*

2. Allow plenty of time for participants to say whatever there is to say about the outcome with no right answers expected and no commenting on what people have said. The objective is to *give everyone a chance to vent* and let go of his or her story about what happened.

3. *Continue the process* until no one has anything more to say.

4. *Bring the participants to choice*—let go of the past and focus on fulfilling our Yonder Star or continue holding on. Ask the following questions:

   ✓ Is everyone "complete"—willing to let go of the situation, project, or goal and move on?
   ✓ Are all of you willing to let the whole event become part of the past?
   ✓ Are you willing to forgive yourself or each other for any shortfalls or upsets that may still be hanging around?
   ✓ Are you ready to engage newly?

From Upset to Productivity— Uncovering and Speaking Commitment

Taking yourself lightly, expanding your Learning Zone, and effectively collaborating with others all require that you build your capacities to recognize and move through your own upsets and those of people around you.

Wouldn't it be valuable to you if:

- you could express yourself calmly and powerfully even when you are very concerned, upset, or fearful;

- you could be considered a thoughtful and passionate person rather than a touchy emotional one;

- people around you would stop whining and complaining and get to work;

- you built a reputation for dealing with difficult and emotional situations and turning them into productive conversations where results get produced and participants experience being valued and valuable?

When something gets in the way of your commitments, goals, or intentions and seems to threaten success, you may find yourself upset, concerned, or fearful. The more intensely you care, the more upset you may get.

Here is the recommended preparation followed by a worksheet to help shift the focus of your thinking and conversations from survival-brain worries, concerns, and fears (the lower line of the Leadership Choice Point) to a place of perspective, power, and productivity (the upper line in the Leadership Choice Point). The process requires self observing, catching yourself and reframing the way you think about and react to upsets, fears, worries, and complaints, whether you are working with your own upset or those of others around you. Once again, it is simple and not easy.

Shifting Your Own Upsets: Uncovering and Speaking Your Commitment

To use the process for yourself, first practice with the worksheet. Then use it to clear yourself when you have a topic or issue that you feel upset about or want to complain about, *before* you enter into that difficult conversation with another. You can also use it to review a failed, unproductive attempt and learn how you might have approached the interaction more effectively. The better you are at using this process for yourself, the better you will be at using it with other people.

Step 1: Be present and notice!
Notice when you are upset, worried, fearful, or complaining. Each person exhibits his or her own symptoms and they can vary based on the situation and people involved.

- Know yourself; know your triggers and your hot buttons.

- Learn to observe and catch yourself in that mode.

- Breathe Out!

- Ask yourself a brain-switching question—switching from survival brain mode to your thinking brain. For example; "What's the bigger picture here?"

- Go to the worksheet to uncover your commitments and to return your power before the next conversation.

Step 2: Get curious and reframe!
Begin to relate to upsets as clues to commitment and to consider upset people (including yourself) as intensely committed. Begin to wonder: What is the commitment in the background that is fueling this upset in the foreground?
Intervene in your "righteous rage of the wronged," your fear of failure, or your avoidance of potentially looking bad. Shift to

considering yourself an intensely committed person, wonder what the intense commitment is that is driving your reaction, and...go to the worksheet!

Step 3: Re-engage at the level of commitment!

When you lead and speak from your commitments (the upper line of the Leadership Choice Point—what you are for) rather than your worries, concerns, and upsets (the lower line of the Leadership Choice Point—what you are against or trying to avoid), you can move the conversation and the energy in a productive direction. You also shift the way people listen to you on the topic and make it easier for them to hear you. Most people find it difficult to listen to and deal with upsets, complaints, and the fears of others in a productive way. You minimize your ability to be heard and appreciated for your perspective when you communicate from your survival brain. Since there is a commitment hidden in every upset, learn to find it and communicate from there. Over time, and with lots of practice, you will notice that you can stop, reframe, and reengage in the middle of your own upset!

Use the following worksheet and process to help recover your thinking brain and speak from your commitments.

Outline and Worksheet Instructions:
For Your Own Upsets!

From Upset to Productivity—Uncovering and Speaking Commitment

Leadership Choice Point

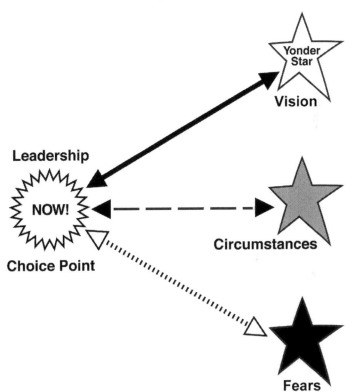

Step 1: Pick an example of something you have been upset about or feel worried, concerned, or fearful about. List the *topic*. It is usually an event, action, or conversation (or the lack of one) rather than a person. Remember to separate the person from the issue. While there is often a person or group associated with your upset, separating the person from the event is critical. If you still think your topic is a person, ask yourself, "What happened with that person?" That is the topic.

Step 2: Next list your *feelings* (not concepts) about the situation. Feelings are usually described with one word each (sad, angry, frustrated, anxious, fearful). This step allows you to identify the key emotions in the upset and become more of an observer of your feelings rather than controlled by them. When it is time to re-engage with another person, you will be able to speak *about* your emotions rather than speaking *from* your emotions.

Step 3: List your worries, concerns, and fears. What can go wrong if this issue isn't handled? What is the worst-case scenario? What are you fearful of? Ask yourself, "So what if that happens?" Write some more. Your intention here is to get the worries, concerns, and fears out of your head and onto paper, which shines a light on them. A fully and deeply explored list of worries and concerns is important for the next step.

Step 4: Review your worries/concerns/fears. Write each statement in the opposite (flip them 180 degrees) to uncover several *possible* commitments, intentions, or a Yonder Star. This is not about being positive. It is a creative process to return to your higher thinking brain—the part that can consider options, use creativity, and engage others in a collaborative manner.

Step 5: Review each of your new statements. Which of them (or combination of them) seems to state what you are most committed to? If you haven't said it accurately, what new statement can you write, spring-boarding from what you currently have, that accurately captures the real essence?

Step 6: Get re-engaged with your thinking brain.
Acknowledge your commitment and share it with others, if appropriate. Acknowledge your emotions around the commitment and share them, if appropriate. If shared, speak about your emotions, not through them! Step into issue identification and brainstorming mode now that you have access to the thinking part of your brain. Include others who can help with identifying solutions or implementing them. Create a new game plan and get into action.

Worksheet: For Your Own Upsets
From Upset to Productivity

1. **Topic (Often the 'trigger')** Example: Missed deadline on the event timeline

   _____

   _____

2. **Feelings/Emotions** Examples: Anxious, concerned, fearful, angry, frustrated

   _____

   _____

3. **Fears—Worries—Concerns** Examples: I/we will look bad. The project/event will fail. The consequences will be unacceptable. I could lose my job/get blamed. *Get underneath, ask so what?* The event won't raise enough money. It will be unprofessional and hurt our brand/reputation. The XYZ program won't be fully funded. The clients won't have full value delivered.

   _____

   _____

4. **Possible Commitments/Yonder Star List** Examples: I/we will display our best. The project/event will be wildly successful. The ripple effect from this event will be favorable for us, and our clients. It will be a contribution to my career experiences. The event will raise plenty of money, fully funding the XYZ program. It will be very professional and our reputation/brand will be enhanced. The clients will be very pleased with the value the event provides. You get the idea…now write yours!

   _____

   _____

Worksheet – Page 2: For Your Own Upsets!
From Upset to Productivity

5. **Choose and Express Your Commitment and Re-Engage with Your Thinking Brain**   Example: I am committed to a highly successful event that accomplishes or even exceeds the goals for our clients and demonstrates our skill and professionalism. I have been very frustrated and even angry about the missed date on our event timeline. I have been anxious and worried that we would still be able to pull it off in a professional and successful manner. It is going to take some creativity and a plan that I haven't already thought of to get us back on track. I am ready to have a conversation for the next actions we can take to pull it off. Write Yours:

_____

_____

_____

_____

_____

_____

Shifting Upsets of Others: Listening to Uncover Commitment

To use this process successfully with others requires that you are able to remain calm and focused in the presence of other people when they are upset, concerned, complaining, or intensely emotional. The most frequent reaction when one person gets upset is that the other person (who was not previously upset) either:

1. Gets upset *along with* the person—colluding with the unfairness or outrageousness of their predicament—which generally leads to both people getting "spun up." Now two people (or more) are caught up in their survival brains and have blocked access to creativity, analysis and reason.

2. Gets upset *at* the person for being so upset or complaining;

   - Takes it as a personal attack or

   - Heaps judgment on the other person for being in that state

   Leading to:

   - Defense or counter attack

   - "Should-ing" on the other person: "You shouldn't be upset." "You shouldn't talk that way." "You should calm down." "It's not really that bad." "There is really nothing to worry about." "Stop complaining."

The end result is escalation, disconnection, and waste. Escalation can also lead to irreparable damage to the relationship and certainly expends a huge amount of energy expanding the issue rather than resolving it.

Consider the escalation of an upset much like a traffic accident. Two vehicles are traveling down the road, one behind the other, when the driver of the car in front slams on its brakes with no warning. The second car slams into the rear of the first car, causing lots of damage to both cars and maybe to the people inside them. In traffic law (in most states), the driver from behind is deemed to be "at fault." "But, officer, he slammed on his breaks with no warning!" Nevertheless, the car traveling behind has the last opportunity to prevent the accident.

And so it is with upsets. When people are upset, many say and do things they probably would not do in their "right mind." When another person is upset and you are not (yet), then, as in the traffic example, you are the last person with the opportunity to prevent an accident and resulting damage (escalation). When you become upset because they are upset, or because of whatever they said or did while they were upset (out of their mind—or out of their thinking mind, anyway) the situation escalates. Consider that you were the last one who had the opportunity to avoid that accident or, said another way; *you were the last one who could grant the other person the opportunity to restore his or her dignity.*

Step 1: Be present and notice!

Notice when another person is upset, seems to be complaining, is expressing their concerns or talking about what they don't want (lower line of the Leadership Choice Point Graphic). Stay present and connected.

Step 2: Get curious and reframe!

Begin to relate to upsets as clues to commitment (Yonder Star) and to consider upset people as intensely committed. Begin to wonder: What is the commitment in the background that is fueling this upset in the foreground?

Shift or reframe your label for the person and the situation from upset, out of control, emotional, or any other similar label, and relate to them as a very committed person whose commitment is currently hidden in their upset. Listen, listen, listen. Use the worksheet to help you discover a process to listen through the upset and complaints (lower line of the Leadership Choice Point) to hear the commitment in the background (upper line of the Leadership Choice Point).

Step 3: Re-engage at the level of commitment!

When you engage with another person as a committed and passionate person and speak their commitment back to them, they feel heard and validated and very often the upset or unproductive emotion de-escalates. Worries, concerns, and fears can be identified, reframed and discussed as roadblocks and potholes to tackle *together* inside the context of the commitment that is being threatened and therefore stirring them up. Facts and data can be explored separately from the emotions tied to them. Required resources can be identified and productive action steps can be developed. Your reputation will build as someone who can handle tough situations, conversations, and people. People will appreciate being around you when they know they can be fully appreciated for their passion and humanity and can get trued up to the bigger picture by interacting with you.

Use the following worksheet and process to play a productive role in helping a person who is currently upset return to their thinking brain. Remember to be sure you are not in reaction or upset mode yourself!

Outline and Worksheet Instructions:
When Others Are Upset!
From Upset to Productivity—Uncovering and Speaking Commitment

Leadership Choice Point

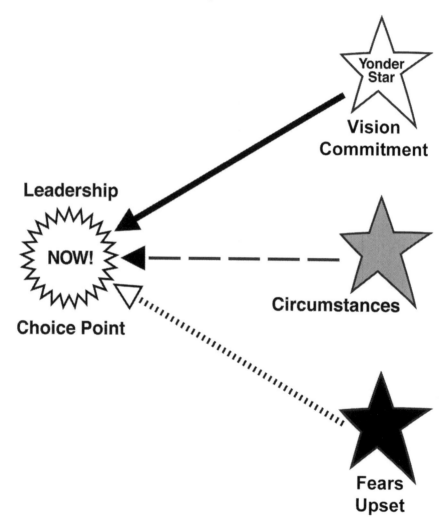

Step 1: Listen for the key content and topical area of the upset. There may be many, so pick one that you can work with during the conversation. It is usually an event, action, or conversation (or the lack

of one) rather than a person. Remember to separate the person from the issue. While there is often a person or group associated with the upset, separating the person from the event is critical. Sometimes it will sound as if *you* are the issue for the other person in an upset. Stay centered, resist the temptation to defend yourself, and listen through what sounds like an attack to what may have caused the upset. People who are upset are not rational…they are in their survival brain!

Step 2: Next listen for the *feelings* (not concepts) that are being expressed about the situation and the intensity of their feelings on a scale of 1-10 where one is low and ten is high. Feelings are usually described with one word each (sad, angry, frustrated, anxious, fearful). You may have heard the other person state these emotions explicitly, more likely you will have to listen beyond what they say and consider what feelings are being expressed. This step in the process allows you to identify the key emotions in the upset which helps you understand how significant it is for the other person and to keep your attention and listening "other focused."

Step 3: List their worries, concerns, and fears. Some may have been explicitly expressed and some you may have picked up from behind the words. You don't have to get it "right" at this point. This list is your perception and interpretation of their fears, concerns and worries. The point of this part of the process is to identify what the concerns and fears seem to be so that you can then uncover a commitment in the background.

Step 4: Review the worries/concerns/fears. Write each statement in the opposite (flip them 180 degrees) to uncover several *possible* commitments, intentions, or a Yonder Star. This is not about being positive. It is a creative process to give you a place to speak from to help return the other person to their higher thinking brain—the part that can consider options, use creativity, and engage others in a collaborative manner.

Step 5: Review each of the new statements. Which of them (or combination of them) seems to state what they may be most committed to?

Step 6: Engage with the other person by acknowledging their commitment. Ask them how you can help further identify the gaps between the present situation and their commitment. What role can you play in the resolution? Step into issue identification and brainstorming mode if you now have access to the thinking part of their brain. Include others who can help with identifying solutions or implementing them. Create a new game plan and get into action.

Step 7: If their upset is not diminished, or if you have become upset, use "I" statements and:

- State your intention to resolve this with them

- Ask to reschedule giving you time to reflect and regroup

Step 8: Before your next conversation have a conversation about your conversations (see prior practical application), then try again to resolve the topic or issue!

Worksheet: When Others Are Upset

1. Topic (Often the 'trigger')

_____

_____

2. Their Feelings/Emotions (Explicit or implicit)

_____

_____

3. Fears—Worries—Concerns

_____

_____

4. Possible Commitments/Yonder Star List:

_____

_____

_____

_____

_____

_____

5. Choose and Express Their Commitment and re-engage with their thinking brain.

Example: I am hearing that you are committed to a highly successful event that accomplishes or even exceeds the goals for our clients *and* demonstrates our skill and professionalism. I am sensing frustration and maybe even some anger about the missed date on our event timeline. I share your concern about being able to pull it off in a professional and successful manner. It is going to take some creativity and a plan that we haven't already thought of to get us back on track. Are you ready to have a conversation for the next actions we can take to pull it off?

Write Yours: _____

_____

_____

6. If their upset is not dimished:

Use "I" statements, state your intention to resolve this with them and ask to reschedule.

EXAMPLE: This topic is important and I want to help get it resolved. I need some time to reflect and a chance to think through some things. Could we arrange to talk again about this (suggest a date)? DO NOT SAY: "Clearly you are upset and in your survival brain so let me know when you are able to have a rational conversation about this!" Escalation is sure to happen! Write something in your own words for practice:

_____

_____

7. Before the next conversation:

See the Practical Application earlier in this section *Have a Conversation About Your Conversations—Building Conversational Capacity.*

Practical Applications

1. The Three Levels of Conversational Impact as a Diagnostic Tool
      A Conversation About Your Conversations
      A Conversation About Your Relationship

2. Questions to Explore Reality—Curiosity versus Interrogation

3. Eliminate the Buts!

4. Unmasking the Issue—Reframing "Wrong"

5. Finding Alignment—Moving the Conversation and the Focus "One Up"

6. Productive Delegation

7. Productive Meetings

8. Project Performance Review

9. Dialogue for Making a Role Change or Closing a Performance Gap

10. Acknowledgement, Appreciation, Celebration and Completion
      If the Project Hasn't Been Fully Completed

11. From Upset to Productivity
      Shifting Your Own Upsets
      Shifting the Upsets of Others

Conclusion

We have now arrived at the beginning. Like the locker room at half time during a sports event, reading this book was not the game, your life is. The value of the book will live or fade in your willingness to practice, fail, and go at it again until the Operating Principles become natural. Lou Tice of the Pacific Institute says to practice until your second nature becomes your first nature. After a while you will begin to notice when one of the principles is missing in a conversation and be able to weave it in quite naturally. Your interactions will become dramatically more productive and others will be looking to you for coaching. When you have really mastered the material, you will think you have always been that way. People around you will be adopting your "approach" because it works.

If you are the kind of person who joins a gym and exercises very rigorously right after New Year's Day and then can't remember when you were there last or is always rushing to finish reading the latest leadership or communication book so you can read yet another on your night stand, you are at great risk of disappointment with the investment you made in reading this book. The good ideas will die as just that – good ideas. As we've said over and over, it's all about getting in the game, practicing, failing, and getting up and going at it again until you have built new capacities, new muscles, and formed new habits. Make promises to others, form a support group, or do whatever you have to do to support yourself in doing the work. Now go get with it, celebrate your accomplishments, no matter how small at first, and have fun!

Glossary

Throughout the text and this section, we refer to a series of graphics. All of those graphics are available in color and in a downloadable pdf format from our Web site, www.2130partners.com.

Acknowledgement: Presence to and expressed awareness of another or others. Also a willingness to recognize and accept a condition or set of circumstances without judgment, e.g., "I acknowledge that the results we were striving for by today were not produced." From this perspective it is recognition of the way that it is and the way that it isn't. May also include an expression of appreciation.

Appreciation: Speaking in a manner that has another feel valued and valuable. Includes expressions of recognition, enjoyment, or gratitude. It is most powerful when it is specific, personal and timely.

Choice: A key leadership act of selecting between two or more possibilities—always in the present moment. A key component of Self-Generated Accountability and alignment.

Collaboration: Interaction with others in an open, sharing, and mutually supportive manner that is intended to further a mutual goal, objective, or vision. It is most effective when participants create an atmosphere of mutual trust, respect, and safety and are willing to be vulnerable. Distinct from *cooperation*, where participants supply just what is requested with a reciprocal expectation.

Completion: Fully claiming the past, releasing any attachments, acknowledging successes and learning, and clearing space for what's next.

Confront: To stand together, in partnership—present to opportunities and challenging obstacles on a shared path—distinct from confronting another person. (See "Productive Dialogue Zone" graphic, page 41.)

Connected: To be in relationship or partnership with others. To have an experience of, and access to, each other's worlds.

Conversational Capacities: Describes the depth of topics or challenges we can address successfully together. Our conversational capacities either expand or shrink with every interaction (See "Three Levels of Conversational Impact" in Essential Notions—Section One, page 35, and see "Productive Dialogue Zone" graphic, page 41.)

Exploration Listening: A manner of listening where you are authentically curious, connected to the other person, open, and focused on what he or she has to say. You are listening beyond the content to understand the emotions and intent of the other person. You are "other-focused" and outside your own Mental File Cabinet.

File Cabinet Brain/Mental File Cabinet: A metaphor representing the way a brain operates as an information management and storage system to perceive, filter, file, retrieve, and use input. The metaphor is then used to demonstrate the source of our mental and emotional barriers to productive interactions.

Friction and Waste: The unnecessary expenditure of energy and loss of time and creativity resulting from slowed, useless, or extremely negative interactions that impede productivity. Costs include gaps and delays in plan execution, flare-ups of unproductive and draining emotions, distrust, unreliable performance, competition, and resignation.

Leadership: Quoting Warren Bennis, "Leadership is the wise use of power. Power is the ability to translate intention into reality and sustain it." Throughout the text we are speaking of leadership qualities—abilities to be present and translate intention— rather than an individual, style, or personality. These qualities may be exhibited by any person in an organization (or family) at any time. We suggest that they will be required of everyone in an organization to succeed and thrive in the unfolding new reality.

Leadership Choice Point: A model we have created to demonstrate the choice that is available to you at each and every moment in life. You can correlate your thoughts and actions with fulfilling your Yonder Star; focus your efforts on continuing your existing reality in its current state; or work to avoid your feared outcomes. In the next moment, you can choose again. The idea is quite simple, while living that way is a lifetime of learning to practice the discipline. (See the "Leadership Choice Point" graphic, page 28.)

Learning Zone: This zone occurs when you are beyond your comfort zone and have not yet stepped into to the distress/survival brain mode. This zone is where you are most able to learn and assimilate new information and experiences into your mental File Cabinet. After enough practice this new learning contributes to development of a newly expanded comfort zone—increased capacities, and strengthened conversational muscles. (See "Emotional Zones" graphic, page 38.)

Levels of Conversational Impact: Topic, capacity, and relationship: When all involved are open, sharing, and productively engaged, topics can be discussed creatively and desired results occur rapidly. If the conversation is not working at the topic level, back up and have a conversation about the conversation—exploring the conversational capacities that are missing or would have to be invoked to get the conversation flowing at the level of topic. If the conversation is still stuck, back up further and have a conversation about the relationship(s). Mutual trust, respect, and safety are the fundamental context for real relationship.

Malicious Compliance: A term contributed by a workshop participant that we now use to describe an undesirable outcome of the command and control management paradigm and when describing a possible outcome of a 'dueling File Cabinet' scenario where the person who usually gets their way is the person with the most power. We say they have 'powered over' the other person, and in return get appeasement rather than engagement. Compliance requires a very low level (if any) real engagement of mental capacity or creativity. Malicious Compliance adds the passive aggressive feeling of "ok sure we'll do it your way" and then they do exactly what you asked, nothing more and nothing less. When the project fails, they are off the hook because they did exactly what you said. There is even a bit of "I told you so, but you wouldn't listen, you had to have it your way" in the background. The opposite of Malicious Compliance is Self-Generated Accountability, unleashed creativity and purposeful engagement.

Mental and Emotional Barriers: These terms capture how thoughts and feelings can hijack your abilities and get in your own way of being more productive. Your past-based filters and stored perceptions influence your experience of "reality" and can trigger your survival brain mode. Triggering leads to disconnection from others, a distorted view of what is actually happening, and crippled ability to generate creative, timely solutions. (Check out our "Dueling File Cabinets" graphic, page 26.)

One Up: An expression that serves as a thought cue to take the conversation and your intention up one level higher than the current level to generate or regenerate alignment. For example, a goal is "one up" from an action; a strategy is "one up" from a goal. (See Vision-Focused Leadership graphic, page 20.)

Operating Principles: A system of premises that cause powerful, productive interventions into conventional thinking, ways of being, and patterns of interaction when practiced until they become new patterns of thinking (we call that "uploading".) They work as a system to support a safe, creative, and productive workspace in which to raise and resolve issues. They require a shift from status quo, all-knowing confidence, rigidity, and judgment to curiosity, connection, mental agility and learning—as well as courage, choice, and practice.

Operating System: Our metaphor referring to the patterns of recorded pictures, experiences, emotions, and conversations that run your mind. In particular we are focused on those patterns of thought which were "loaded in" when you were very young, which are now mostly subconscious, and which still control many of your actions and reactions to others.

Operating System Upgrades: A metaphor referring to your individual opportunity to "upload,'" "upgrade," and "update" your thinking processes to more fully equip yourself to work effectively and interact productively in the emerging new reality—one that is more complex, fast paced, and dynamically changing today than ever before.

Potholes: A metaphor used to describe a gap in resources, actions, or interactions that you will be required to 'fill in' on the way to accomplishing your shared vision, objectives or goals. (See the "Productive Dialogue" graphic, page 20.)

Productive: Useful to achieving your shared vision, objectives, or goals, and generally to building stronger, more effective, and enjoyable relationships.

Productive Dialogue: A conversation where individual and mutual realities are explored and new ideas and solutions are generated that did not exist prior to the conversation. These are interactions that take place in an environment where participants feel safe enough to really investigate their own and others' realties and take responsibility for making the dialogue a success. Operating principles are being embraced and observed.

Productive Dialogue Zone: The conversational arena where both connection to others and real issues are being confronted simultaneously. Participants are being direct *and* sensitive; they get results *and* enhance relationship. Mutual trust, respect and safety are present. (See the "Productive Dialogue Zone" graphic, page 41.)

Productive Environment: A conversational workspace that facilitates creative interactions and allows the effectiveness of interactions to be maximized. The Operating Principles are in play and the atmosphere is one of mutual trust, respect, and safety where contributions are valued and participants can provide input without fear of ridicule or retribution.

Real Issues: The issues, often the ones being avoided or obscured, that must be confronted individually and as a team to effectively accomplish your shared goals and objectives. Real issues are "road blocks" and "potholes" between your current situation and your goal or Yonder Star. When avoided, discussions often get sidetracked or distracted onto issues of right, wrong, blame, judgment, or seeing each other as the issue. This sets up opposition within the team and drains productivity and creative energy.

Reality: Present circumstances, conditions, and perceptions, the naming and labeling of which is explored and identified from many perspectives. Absence of blame or judgment allows the greatest opportunity for value in problem solving.

Responsible: The act of considering oneself capable and charged with being present, at choice, and able to respond versus react. As is regularly said throughout the ancient I Ching, "No blame."

Roadblocks: Obstacles or unsolved issues in the path between your goals and objectives and the present moment. People are not roadblocks, though some of their behaviors might be.

Safe: An environment or relationship in which each person's contributions are considered valid and valuable by others who have chosen to view them that way. Conflicting perspectives can be explored for contribution to solutions rather than attacked or defended.

Self-Generated Accountability: An act of stepping up and taking personal responsibility for your actions, decisions and communications. Shifting the source and responsibility for raising and resolving issues and producing results from "out there" to "in here." "I am the boss of me!" as our two-year-old wise advisor passed on to us.

Sensitive: Highly aware of the attitudes and feelings of others.

Successful Collaboration: There are several essential ways of being to keep in mind as you develop your collaborative skills, including and not limited to:

- ✓ aligning and focusing on a shared Yonder Star;
- ✓ creating an atmosphere of mutual trust, respect, and safety;
- ✓ openly sharing knowledge, information, and resources;
- ✓ generating forward movement with clarity and accountability;
- ✓ connecting to one another and interacting as team members, openly sharing skills, resources and creativity—going beyond negotiating or cooperating, as in "I'll give you what you want (but not more) if you give me what I want."

Survival Brain Mode: In the distress mode, unproductive emotions are generated, attack-defend language is used, and disconnection occurs. Avoidance, freeze, or appease behaviors and other survival tendencies get triggered when this primitive part of our brain takes over. Numerous unhealthy chemical reactions take place that can lead to stress claims and illness.

truths: Only your perspective, your own reality, not universal truth or absolutes.

Up and Out: A very useful "brain-switching" statement when you find yourself stuck in the topic or discussion at hand. It helps move away from dueling File Cabinet minds. Visualize looking up and out to the horizon and your next higher goal or your Yonder Star itself.

Looking back from there and inviting others to do so with you will generally give a different view and open up creative dialogue.

Vicious Obedience: See Malicious Compliance!

Vision-Focused Leadership™: The context, or model, we employ to replace the older command-and-control paradigm. This mental model shows how your thinking, listening, speaking, and actions (most importantly those that you employ to lead others) are focused and informed by a shared vision. Focusing on a shared vision in the present moment allows you to make choices, orient your creativity, energy, and resources, and align your actions and the actions of those working with you on what you intend to produce together rather than where you have been. One of the most important aspects of this conversation is securing the creative energy and input of the entire team rather than everyone standing around waiting for their actions and orders from the commanding officer. In the absence of shared vision, it is common to source your actions in your self-concept and worldview, which are pretty much past based. It is easy to become a victim to or be distracted by circumstances, worries, and fears—reacting from your brain's instant, automatic, unconscious, and unexamined impulses. (See "Vision-Focused Leadership graphic, page 20.)

Index

A

Accelerate: *High Leverage Leadership for Today's World*
  authors' intention for, xxii, 1–2
  contacting the authors, 339
  glossary, 307–313
  testimonials, iii–v
  YouTube video clips from, 339
Accountability, 56–57, 248–256. *See also* Self-Generated Accountability
Acknowledgement
  defined, 307
  of your own commitment, 292
Acknowledgement, Appreciation, Celebration and Completion (Practical Application #10), 280–284
  Operating Principles emphasized in, 283
Action Science (Argyris), 107
Actions
  choosing, 246
  correlated with circumstances, 29–31
  language that discourages, 113
  leveraged, 21
  relationship with goals, 244
Active listening, 297
Adams, Marilee, *Change Your Questions, Change Your Life*, 114–115

Agreeing to disagree, 136
Alignment, 266–270. *See also* Collaboration; Finding Alignment (Practical Application #5); Shared vision
"and," using instead of "but," 153, 234–236. *See also* Eliminate the Buts! (Practical Application #3)
Appeasing, 37, 196, 199. *See also* Avoidance; Malicious Compliance
Appreciation of others, 280–284
  defined, 307
Argyris, Chris, 107
Avoidance
  about, 199
  by using Nothing is Wrong or Broken Operating Principle, 121
  case study about, 189
  impact on results, 43
  of real issues, 147
  See also Appeasing

B

"bad news" bearers, 191
Batchelder, Tom, *Barking Up a Dead Horse*, 134–138
Be Direct and Sensitive (Operating Principle). *See* Direct; Sensitive
Be Present, Stay in the Game (Operating Principle #1), 62–77

Be Present, Stay in the Game
(continued)
case study: Learning to Connect, 75
case study: Suzanne - Shocked to
Attention, 76
Practice Opportunities: Being
Present in Your Daily Life, 77
See also Presence; Staying in the
Game
Be Responsible for Creating Value
(Operating Principle #7), 164–174
case study: Dwight - Taming my File
Cabinet, 172
case study: Dwight - Who's Bringing
the Value?, 173
Practice Opportunities: Bring
Attention to Your Intention, 174
See also Responsibility
Be Responsible for What Gets Heard
(Operating Principle #9), 192–206
case study: Be Right or Be Effective,
204
Practice Opportunities: Check How
the Message Landed, 206
Practice Opportunities:
Communicate with a Clean
and Clear Intention, 205
See also Productive Dialogue;
Responsibility; Self-Generated
Accountability
Beliefs. See truths
Bennis, Warren, quoted, 308
Bergquist, Jim (Business Futures
Consulting), 48–49
Blaming, 115–117
Body language, 199–200

Boss of Me (I am The), 59, 167
Build on the Participation of Others
(Operating Principle), 173, 179–180
Building Collaborative Capital
Requires Relationship and
Confrontation (Essential Notions),
9–11, 34–44
Burger, Jerry, obedience experiments,
23–24
"but," replacing with "and," 153,
234–236. See also Eliminate the
Buts! (Practical Application #3)

C

Celebration of results, 280–284
Change Your Questions, Change Your
Life (Adams), 114–115
Changing others, 50–51
Changing your mind, 80–81
Choice
choice points, 63
defined, 307
Operating Principles' need for, 52
See also Leadership Choice Point
Circumstances
living under past or current, 29–31,
33
Clarity at project performance
reviews, 266–270
Collaboration
defined, 307
developing skill at, 287
effective, 129
foundation for building, 177
improving, 136–137

Collaboration (*continued*)
  role of Productive Dialogue, 40
  successful collaboration defined, 312
  Vision-Focused Leadership and, 17–18
  See also Alignment
Collaborative capacities, 44
  in Productive Dialogue Zone, 162
Collaborative capital, 44, 162, 186
Comfort Zone, 38
Command and control management
    paradigm, 6–7, 23. *See also*
    Vision-Focused Leadership
Commitment
  mutual commitment in
    Conversations about
    Relationships, 222
  to uncover a shared reality, 133
  uncovering and speaking other's,
    289–294
  uncovering and speaking your own,
    289–294
Completion
  defined, 307
  of projects, 280–284
Concentration. *See* Focus
Concerns
  working with other people's, 299
  working with your own, 292
Confidence-building, 248–256
Confirmation bias, 107
Confront and Deal with Real Issues
    (Operating Principle #6), 144–156
  case study: Scarcity - The Real Issue,
    154
  Practice Opportunities: Will the Real
    Issue Please Stand Up?, 155

Confronting
  defined, 42, 145, 307
  failing team members, 266–270
  issues rather than people, 43
  less than stellar results from a team,
    284
  See also Courage; Productive
    Dialogue Zone
Connecting, 42, 43
  defined, 307
  Successful Collaboration and, 312
  See also Disconnected listening;
    Productive Dialogue Zone
Connolly, Mickey (Conversant
    Solutions), 166
"Contingency Life" (Whyte), 31
Conversational Capacities, 36, 39
  building your own, 212–216
  defined, 307–308
  improving by exploring *truths*, 136
Conversations
  designing, 47–51
  effective, 168–169
  with failing team members,
    266–270
  how to have productive, 211–212
  moving them "One Up," 242–247
  that shape our world, 27
  See also Be Responsible for What
    Gets Heard (Operating Principle
    #9); Conversations about
    Conversations; Conversations
    about Relationships; Listening;
    Productive Dialogue; Productive
    Dialogue Zone; Questions; Three
    Levels of Conversational Impact

Conversations about Conversations
building conversational capacities,
212–216
to get at real issues, 150–151
when an upset not diminished,
300
when delegating, 252–253
worksheet, 217
Conversations about Relationships,
213
building mutual trust, respect, and
safety, 218–223
worksheet, 224
Cooperation, 307. *See also*
Collaboration
Costs
of dysfunctional workplaces, 8–9
of Friction and Waste, 308
of rigidity, 139
"could," using instead of "should,"
116–117, 236
Courage, 32, 42
case study about, 99
Operating Principles' need for, 52
in Productive Dialogue, 162
See also Confronting; Productive
Dialogue Zone
Curiosity, 79–80
case study about, 87
deal with "convince and convert"
mode with, 121–122
deal with your own upset with,
289–290
versus interrogation, 226–233
shifting towards, 235–236

D

Death by Meetings (Lencione), 259
Decision-making, 231–233
Declarations, 111–113
about your own reality, 132
for Conversations about
Conversations, 215
defined, 111
regarding performance gap or job/
role changes, 276
self-disclosures, 215–216
that reframe "wrong," 241
that use phrase "here and now,"
122–123
U.S. Declaration of Independence,
112
words to avoid in, 113–119,
120–121
See also "I" statements; Questions
Declare That Each Person's
Contributions are Valid and
Valuable (Operating Principle),
134–138, 179
Declare There is Nothing Wrong or
Broken *Here and Now* (Operating
Principle #4), 110–127, 239
case study: In Spec or Not in Spec?,
125
Practice Opportunities: Learn to
Reframe Productively, 126–127
Dialogue, defined, 160
Dialogue for Making a Role Change
or Closing a Performance Gap
(Practical Application #9), 272–278
Operating Principles emphasized
in, 274

Difficult Conversations: How to Discuss What Matters Most (Heen and Stone), 163

Direct
  defined, 180
  Practice Opportunities for balancing with sensitivity, 188–189
  at project performance reviews, 268
  relationship with Productive Environment, 180–183
Disconnected listening, 82–84
Disconnected speaking, 194–195
"dishtowel story," 180
Distress-Upset Zone, 38–39
  taking yourself lightly and, 95–96
  using reframing to leave, 239–241
  See also Upsets
Dueling File Cabinets, 25–26, 107–108. *See also* Malicious Compliance; Up and Out
Dueling realities, 107–109

E

Either/or thinking, shifting away from, 235
"elephant in the room," 147
Eliminate the Buts! (Practical Application #3), 234–236
Employees. *See* Teams
Engagement
  in meetings, 258–264
  in Productive Dialogue, 158–163
Essential Notions, 6–44
  about, 13–15
  by name, 15

categories, 6–11
conversational impact and, 211–212
importance to productive delegation, 249
purpose, 159
See also Operating Principles; Practical Applications
Exploration Listening, 79–80
  defined, 308
Explore *truths*: Mine, Theirs, and Ours (Operating Principle #5), 128–142
  case study: New File Cabinet - New Relationship, 140–141
  case study: The Cost of Rigidity, 139
  Practice Opportunities: Create a Breakthrough, 142
  Practice Opportunities: Get Really Good at Asking Exploring Questions, 142
  See also Shared vision; *truths*; Understanding perspectives of Others

F

Failure
  case study about, 99
Fears
  focus on, 29
  Leadership Choice Point and, 308
  working with other people's, 299
  working with your own, 292
Feedback, 200–201, 206
Feelings
  identifying and describing your own, 292

Feelings (*continued*)
    listening for others', 299
    See also Three Emotional Zones
Fierce Conversations (Scott), 196
Fifth Discipline, The (Senge), 107
File Cabinet Brain. *See* Mental File
    Cabinet
Finding Alignment (Practical
    Application #5), 242–247
    Operating Principles emphasized
        in, 245
Focus
    fear-based, 29
    on the future, 65–66, 122–123
    moving it "One Up," 242–247
    on the past, 64–65, 122–123
    Yonder Star, 19, 32–33
Four Agreements, The (Ruiz), 93
Friction and Waste
    causes, 193
    defined, 308
    in workplaces, 8–9
Frindt, Dwight R., xvii–xviii, xx–xxi, 337
Frindt, Suzanne Mayo, xix–xxi, 337
From Upset to Productivity (Practical
    Application #11), 286–302
    worksheet - when you are upset,
        293–294
    worksheet: when others are upset,
        301–302
Frustration, 195–196

G

Getting in the Game. *See* Staying in
    the Game

Goals
    celebrating milestones, 283–284
    in Conversations about
        Relationships, 222
    relationship with actions and
        strategies, 244
    restating, 246
    See also Intended Outcomes list;
        Results; Up and Out; Yonder Star
Goleman, Daniel, *Social Intelligence*,
    8, 50
"grand inquisitor" approach, 200
Gratitude. *See* Appreciation
Gray, John, quoted, 94
Groups
    with "clubhouse rules," 48
    interactions in unproductive, 243
    questions for exploring truths, 233
    value creation within, 165–166
    See also Meetings; Teams

H

Heen, Sheila, *Difficult Conversations*, 163
Human mind
    retraining it to aim for Yonder Star, 122
    science of, 50, 51
    See also Mental File Cabinet; Mind-
        set; Operating System Upgrade
Humility, 92
Humor
    case study about, 100
    at others' expense, 92, 93
    Practice Opportunities, 102
Hunger Project, xvii–xviii, xx–xxi
Hurst, Ellen, 335

I

"I agree" and "I disagree," 118–119
"I" Statements
    presence and, 69–70
    Self-Management Practice, 132
    that use phrase "for me," 253
    when upset has not been
        diminished, 302
    See also Declarations
Inquisition of others, 200–201
Intended Outcomes list, 262–264
    for dialogue about performance
        gap or job/role change, 275
Intentions
    "clear" and "clean," 205
    Practice Opportunities for
        attending to your own, 173
    uncovering other people's, 299
    uncovering your own, 292
    and value creation, 168–169
    See also Intended Outcomes list
Internal conversations, 82–84
Interruptions, dealing with your own,
    190
"investigative vulnerability, an"
    (Whyte), 47
Isolation ("creeping disconnection"), 8
Issues, 36
    confronting, 145–146
    depersonalizing, 291–292, 299
    getting at the real, 147–149, 156, 297
    "real issues" defined, 311
    separating your emotions from, 96
    that create roadblocks and
        potholes, 146–147

unmasking the real issues, 149–150
    See also Appeasing; Avoidance;
        Confront and Deal with Real
        Issues (Operating Principle #6)
It Begins with Me, 54–60

J

Johnson, Spencer, *Who Moved My
    Cheese*, 65
Judging
    choosing responsibility over, 172
    public speakers, 169
    reducing your own tendency
        toward, 126–127
    as sign value-creation responsibility
        is missing, 170–171
    using the concept of "wrong,"
        113–122
    while listening, 82–84
    yourself, 91–92

K

"killing the messenger," 191
Konstanturos, John (Continuous
    Renewal Consulting), 131

L

Ladder of Inference (Argyris), 107
Language
    creative acts in, 111–113
    threatening, 94–96
    "wanna-be," 113

Leadership
  collaborative, 186
  defined, 308
  leveraging your, 188
  who can evoke, 18
  See also Vision-Focused Leadership
Leadership Choice Point, 27–33, 308
  diagram, 28
  getting off the lower line, 239–241,
    287–288, 298
  leading and speaking from the
    upper line, 290, 291
  operating on the upper line, 282
  presence and, 63–65
  between "victim" or "Boss of Me," 167
  and the word "wrong," 114–115
  Yonder Star focus and, 32
  See also Circumstances; Fears;
    Yonder Star
Learning Zone, 38
  defined, 309
  expanding a group's, 169, 170
  expanding your own, 287
Lencione, Patrick, *Death by Meetings*,
  259
Levels of Conversational Impact. *See*
  Three Levels of Conversational
  Impact
Listen Newly, Be Intentionally Slow to
  Understand (Operating Principle
  #2), 78–88
  case study: Cold Case Reopened, 87
  case study: Suzanne - Uncovering a
    Common Yonder Star, 88
  Practice Opportunities, 89

  See also Understanding
    perspectives of others
Listening
  doing it well, 197–198
  "generative" versus "consumptive," 166
  to uncover commitment, 295–302
  See also Exploration Listening

M

Make it Safe *and* Productive
  (Operating Principle #8), 176–191
  case study: Dwight - Let it in and
    Learn, 187
  case study: From Competitive to
    Effective, 186
  Practice Opportunities: Pick Your
    Scenario and Get to Work!,
    188–191
  See also Productive Environment;
    Safety
Malicious Compliance, 24, 42
  defined, 309
  See also Appeasing; Dueling File
    Cabinets; Self-Generated
    Accountability
Meetings, 251–253, 258–264. *See also*
  Groups; Productive Meetings
  (Practical Application #7); Teams
Mental and Emotional Barriers,
  309–310. *See also* Feelings; Three
  Emotional Zones
Mental File Cabinet, 25–26
  checking new information against,
    131–133
  controlling and changing, 80–81

Mental File Cabinet (*continued*)
  creating a new relationship by examining contents, 140–141
  defined, 308
  focusing elsewhere, 84–85
  how Operating Principles affect, 51–52
  Productive Dialogue and, 179
  recognizing other people's, 93
  "what ifs," 66–68
  See also Dueling File Cabinets; Fears; Learning Zone; Potholes; Roadblocks
Milgram, Stanley, obedience experiments, 23–24
'Mind the Gap' warnings, 119
Mind-set
  how to intervene in your usual, 170
  scarcity, 154
  value creation, 166
  See also Reframing
Missions, relationship with goals, 244
Misunderstandings, 193, 195
Mullin, Tom, quoted, 80
Murray, Pat, vii
Mutual trust
  building, through Conversations about Relationships, 218–223
  improving productivity with, 177–179

N

New Nature of Leadership – Replacing Commands with Vision (Essential Notions), 6–7, 16–19

New Ways of Working Together (Essential Notions), 7–9, 22–33

O

Obedience experiments, 23–24. *See also* Malicious Compliance
Objectives. *See* Goals
One Up, 21, 242–247
  defined, 310
Operating Principles, 46–206
  about, 46–53
  by name, 53
  defined, 47, 310
  getting in the game by practicing, 305
  how to use, 114
  origins, vii
  principle, defined, 47
  purpose, 159
  that contribute to creating a safe environment, 179
  using, to get at real issues, 148–149
  See also Essential Notions; Practical Applications
Operating System, 310
Operating System Upgrade, 10–11, 183, 310. *See also* Essential Notions; Operating Principles
Outcomes
  best possible, 114
  engagement at meetings and, 258–264
  how Operating Principles bring about new ones, 51–52

Outcomes (*continued*)
 See also Completion; Intended
  Outcomes list; Results
Own My Own Perception and
 My Participation (Operating
 Principle). *See* "I" statements;
 Participation

P

Pachamama Alliance, xx
"Parking Lot" list, 262, 264
Participation
 other's, 173, 179–180
 your own, 174
Perception. *See* Be Responsible for
 What Gets Heard (Operating
 Principle #9)
Personal responsibility. *See* Self-
 Generated Accountability
Perspective. *See* Point of view
Point of view
 being wedded to your own, 91
 construction site example, 132–133
 truth and, 130
 See also Understanding
  perspectives of others
Potholes, 146–147
 defined, 310
 moving beyond, 160
Power of expectation, 107
Practical Applications, 208–303
 by name, 303
 See also Essential Notions;
  Operating Principles; Self-
  Management Practices

Praise. *See* Acknowledgement
Presence, 66–74, 289
 in the "here and now," 122–123
 Operating Principles' need for, 52
 Survival-brain thinking and, 94–96
 See also Be Present, Stay in the
  Game (Operating Principle #1)
Priming effect, 107
Principles. *See* Operating Principles
Problem-solving, 235–236. *See also*
  Alignment; Outcomes
Productive, defined, 310
Productive Delegation (Practical
 Application #6), 248–256
 Operating Principles emphasized
  in, 249
 preparation form, 256
Productive Dialogue
 about, 159–161
 defined, 40, 311
 using to move One Up, 21
 See also Productive Dialogue Zone;
  Questions
Productive Dialogue Zone, 41–44,
  161–163, 273–274
 defined, 311
 diagram, 41, 181–182
 using, for project performance
  reviews, 267–268
Productive Environment, 20–21,
  177–183. *See also* Make it Safe *And*
  Productive (Operating Principle #8)
Productive Interactions Program, 82
Productive Meetings (Practical
  Application #7), 258–264

Productive Meetings (*continued*)
  Operating Principles emphasized in, 259
  worksheet, 264
Project Performance Review (Practical Application #8), 249, 266–270
  Operating Principles emphasized in, 267
Project reviews, 121
Projects
  course corrections, 255
  at the end of, 253–254
  "off-track," 228–230
  See also Completion; Productive Delegation (Practical Application #6)
Public speaking, 169. *See also* Productive Dialogue
Purpose and Intended Outcomes document, 262–264
Purpose statement, 263

Q

Questions
  to ask about working together better, 216
  asking, at meetings, 252
  brain-switching, 289
  clarifying issues with, 149
  exploring reality with, 142
  exploring *truths* with, 135
  to inquire, explore and connect, 246–247
  to obtain feedback, 200–201, 202, 206
  for productive delegation, 250–251
  for productive meetings, 260–261
  See also Declarations
Questions to Explore Reality (Practical Application #2), 226–233, 249
  Operating Principles emphasized in, 227

R

"reaction mode," 29
Real Issues. *See* Issues
"realistic" expectations, 33
Reality, defined, 311
Reality checks, 104–109
Recognition. *See* Acknowledgement; Appreciation
Re-engaging
  at the level of commitment, 290, 297
  someone else's thinking brain, 302
  your own thinking brain, 294
Reframing
  for dealing with your own upset, 289–290
  the notion of "wrong," 126–127, 238–241
Relationships
  quality, 36–37
  in relation to results, 42–44
  See also Connecting; Productive Dialogue
Reliability versus accountability, 56
Respect
  building, through Conversations about Relationships, 218–223
  improving productivity with, 177–179
Responsibility
  defined, 311

Responsibility (*continued*)
  as a listener, 198
  See also Be Responsible for Creating
    Value (Operating Principle #7);
    Be Responsible for What Gets
    Heard (Operating Principle #9)
Results
  acknowledgement, appreciation
    and celebration of, 280–284
  creating a breakthrough to get, 142
  gap between Yonder Star and, 154
  in relation to relationships, 42–44
  See also Completion; Goals;
    Outcomes
Rianoshek, Richard (Conversant
    Solutions), 166
Right, insisting on being, 202, 204
Roadblocks, 146–147
  defined, 311
  moving beyond, 160
Root cause analysis, 121
Ruiz, Don Miguel, *The Four
    Agreements*, 92–93
Rules versus Operating Principles, 48

S

Safe, defined, 312
Safety
  building, through Conversations
    about Relationships, 218–223
  defined, 177
  how you can create, 179
  to improve productivity, 177–179
  relationship with "Direct" and
    "Sensitive," 180–183

  See also Make it Safe *and* Productive
    (Operating Principle #8)
Scarcity mind-set, 154
Schema Theory, 107
Scott, Susan, *Fierce Conversations*,
  196
Self-Generated Accountability
  about, 23–26, 55–60
  and Be Responsible for What Gets
    Heard (Operating Principle #9),
    194, 201–202
  in Conversations about
    Relationships, 222
  creating value with, 165–166
  defined, 312
  for others' reactions to us, 51
  Practice Opportunities for building,
    188–191
  and Taking Myself Lightly
    (Operating Principle #3), 92–93
  See also Malicious Compliance
Self-judgments, 91–92
Self-Management Practices
  Avoiding "I agree" or "I disagree," 118
  Being Responsible for Creating
    Value, 167
  Catch Yourself in "Convince and
    Convert" Mode, 120–121
  Dealing with a "Heavy" Issue, 96
  Don't Should on Me!, 116–117
  "I" Statements, 132
  Listening Fully, 82
  A Pitfall to Watch For: Deflecting
    Blame, 121
  See also Practical Applications
Senge, Peter, *The Fifth Discipline*, 107

Sensitive
  defined, 180, 312
  Practice Opportunities for balance-
    ing with directness, 188–189
  during project performance
    reviews, 268
  relationship with Productive
    Environment, 180–183
Shared declarations, 112
"shared social identity," 18
Shared truths
  questions for exploring, 230
  quickest ways to create, 131
Shared vision
  barriers to, 25–26
  importance to Vision-Focused
    Leadership, 17–18
  Yonder Star and, 18–19
  See also Alignment
Shift Happens (YouTube video),
    5, 10
"should," replacing with "could,"
    116–117, 236
Silence, 201
"social brain," 50
Social Intelligence (Goleman), 8, 50
Social isolation, 7–8
Social Safety Conversations –
    Relationship over Results, 43
Solutions. *See* Results
Soul of Money, The (Twist), 27
Speaking. *See* Disconnected speaking;
    Public Speaking
Staying in the Game, 62–77
  by practicing the Operating
    Principles, 305

  getting back into the game, 69
  "sticks and stones," 95
Stone, Doug, *Difficult Conversations*, 163
Strategic Intent, xxii
Strategy, relationships with goals,
    Missions and visions, 244
Stress, 94
Survival-brain
  catching it in yourself, 101
  defined, 312
  sending others into their own,
    195–197
  using reframing to escape, 239
  way of thinking, 94–96

T

Take Myself Lightly (Operating
    Principle #3), 90–102
  case study: A Knife Through the
    Heart, 100
  case study: Dwight - Staying Sane in
    a Storm, 99
  Practice Opportunities: Catching
    Survival-Brain Mode, 101
  Practice Opportunities: Sarcasm to
    Clarity, 102
Taking one's self lightly, 287
  depersonalizing issues, 291–292, 299
Taking things personally, 92–93
Teams
  clarity and alignment with
    members, 266–270
  increases in productivity, 7–9
  involving in planning for
    celebrations, 283

Teams (*continued*)

    making a role change or closing a performance gap, 272–278

    value creation by, 173

    working in the Productive Dialogue Zone, 162

    See also Groups; Meetings

Three Emotional Zones, 37–39

    diagram, 38

    See also Feelings; Upsets

Three Levels of Conversational Impact, 35–39

    defined, 309

    diagram, 35

    using, to get at real issues, 150–151

Three Levels of Conversational Impact as a Diagnostic Tool (Practical Application #1), 210–224

    Operating Principles emphasized in, 213, 218

Tice, Lou (Pacific Institute), 305

Traffic accident example of escalation of upset, 296

Transaction Based Conversations – Results over Relationships, 42

Trust. *See* Mutual trust

truths, 129

    defined, 130, 312

    exploring other people's, 134–135

    exploring your own, 130–133

    questions for exploring, 135, 228–233

    See also Explore *truths*: Mine, Theirs, and Ours (Operating Principle #5); Understanding perspectives of others

Twist, Lynne, *The Soul of Money*, 27

2130 Partners, xx

    about, 307

    downloadable color graphics available on web site, 307

    Facebook page, 339

U

Understanding perspectives of others, 89, 107–109

    versus "convince and convert" mode, 120–121

    instead of seeking *truths*, 130–133

    See also Listen Newly, Be Intentionally Slow to Understand (Operating Principle #2); *truths*

Unmasking the Issue (Practical Application #4), 238–241

    Operating Principles emphasized in, 240

Up and Out, 269–270

    brain-switching questions to get, 289

    defined, 312–313

Upsets

    dealing with, 151

    importance of learning to recognize and move through, 287–288

    sharing your feelings about, 96

    shifting other people's, 295–302

    shifting your own, 289–294

    See also Distress-Upset Zone; From Upset to Productivity (Practical Application #11); Three Emotional Zones

"Use Your Words, people, use your words," 117–119

V

Validation of others, 108, 297. *See also* Declare That Each Person's Contributions are Valid and Valuable (Operating Principle)
Value creation, 165–166, 168–169. *See also* Be Responsible for Creating Value (Operating Principle #7)
Verbal pollution, 113
Version, defined, 130
Viewpoint. *See* Point of view
Vision
  defined, 17
  relationship with goals, 244
  See also Shared vision; Yonder Star
Vision-Focused Leadership, 17–18, 242–245
  defined, 313
  diagram, 178
  foundation for, 177–179
  "good stress" results, 282
  See also Command and control management paradigm
Vistage International, Inc., xx, 337

W

Who Moved My Cheese (Johnson), 65
Whyte, David
  "an investigative vulnerability," 47
  "Contingency Life," 31
  on courage, 32

Working together. *See* New Ways of Working Together (Essential Notions); Shared vision
Worries
  working with other people's, 299
  working with your own, 292
Wrong
  reframing, 126–127
  what's wrong with wrong, 113–122
  See also Declare There is Nothing Wrong or Broken Here (Operating Principle #4)

Y

Yonder Star
  case study about, 88
  creating a mini, 69, 77
  gap between current results and, 154
  getting at real issues with, 147
  hierarchy of Yonder Stars, 244
  how to see, 32–33
  'Mind the Gap' warnings, 119
  presence and, 65
  reality checks and, 106
  shared vision and, 18–19
  taking yourself lightly and focusing on, 97
  uncovering someone else's, 299
  uncovering your own, 292
  using, for conversations with your team members, 275
  using, to displace defensiveness, 187

Yonder Star (*continued*)
    as way of "talking to the puppet" or
        doll, 278

when focus has shifted from, 153
See also Vision-Focused Leadership

Suggested Readings

Five Questions that Change Everything: Life lessons at Work–John J. Sherer, 2008, Word Keepers Inc., Published by Bibliocast, Fort Collins, CO.

The Communication Catalyst: The Fast (But Not Stupid) Track to Value for Customers, Investors, and Employees–Mickey Connoly and Richard Rianoshek, PhD; 2002, Dearborn Trade Publishing, Chicago, IL.

Difficult Conversations: How to Discuss What Matters Most–Douglas Stone, Bruce Patton, Sheila Heen; 1999, Penguin Putnam Inc., New York, NY.

Fierce Conversations: Achieving Success at Work and Life, One Conversation at a Time–Susan Scott; 2002, Penguin Group, New York, NY.

Communicate or Die–Thomas D. Zweifel, Ph.D; 2003, SelectBooks, Inc., New York, NY.

Man's Search for Meaning–Dr. Viktor Frankl; 1984, Washington Square Press, New York, NY.

Think & Grow Rich–Napoleon Hill; 1960, Highroads Media Inc., Los Angeles, CA.

The Power of Now: A Guide to Spiritual Enlightenment–Eckhart Tolle; 1999, Namaste Publishing, Vancouver, B.C., Canada.

A New Earth: Awakening to Your Life's Purpose–Eckhart Tolle; 2005, Penguin Group, New York, NY.

The Soul of Money: Reclaiming the Wealth of Our Inner Resources–Lynne Twist; 2003, W. W. Norton & Co, Inc.. NY.

Life at the Frontier: Leadership through Courageous Conversations (2 CD set)–David Whyte; 2004, Many Rivers Press, Langley, Washington.

The Art of Possibility Transforming Professional and Personal Life–Zander & Zander; 2003, Harvard Business School Press, Boston, MA

Tribal Leadership: Leveraging Natural Groups to Build a Thriving Organization; David Logan, John King and Halee Fischer-Wright; 2008, HarperCollins Publishers, New York, NY.

The Four Agreements–Don Miguel Ruiz; 1997, Amber-Allen Publishing, Inc., San Rafael, CA.

Social Intelligence–Daniel Goleman; 2004, Bantam Dell–a Division of Random House.

Power vs. Force: The Hidden Determinants of Human Behavior–David R. Hawkins, MD, PhD; 2002, Hay House Inc., Carlsbad, CA.

Managing Thought: How Do Your Thoughts Rule Your World?–Mary J. Lore; 2008, Fern Press, Northville, MI.

Thrive!–Standing on Your Own Two Feet in a Borderless World–Mike Cook; 2006, St. Lynn's Press, Pittsburgh, PA.

Change Your Questions Change Your Life: 7 powerful tools for life and work–Marilee Adams PhD; 2004, Berrett-Koehler Publishers, Inc., San Francisco, CA.

Play to Win: Choosing Growth Over Fear in Work and Life–Larry Wilson, Hersch Wilson; 2004, BRAD Press.

Living at the Summit: A Novel Approach To An Exceptional Life–Dr. Tom Hill.

Your Life as Art–Robert Fritz; 2003, Newfane Press, Newfane, VT.

Cracking the Personality Code–Dana Borowka, MA. and Ellen Borowka, MA; 2008, BookSurge.

Barking Up a Dead Horse: Avoiding the Wasted Time and Effort in Business-to-Business Sales; Tom Batchelder; 2007, Dog Ear Publishing, Indianapolis, IN.

Life of Pi–Chapter 56 on Fear; Yann Martel; 2001, Harcourt Inc. Orlando, FL.

About 2130 Partners

Suzanne Mayo Frindt and Dwight Frindt are co-founders of 2130 Partners, a leadership development and education firm founded in 1990. The name 2130 Partners, and the company's core philosophy are derived from a Native American insight, (often attributed to the Iroquois Confederacy), that leaders are accountable in their decision-making for their impact on each of the next seven generations. Seven generations or 140 years from founding is the year 2130. Thus began 2130 Partners' commitment to working from a long term, vision-focused perspective in all of our work.

2130 Partners is dedicated to facilitating executive leadership potential using Vision-Focused Leadership, a methodology grounded in shared vision and built through collaboration. One of the early 2130 colleagues, Ellen Hurst initiated an inquiry that keeps us trued up to our vision on an ongoing basis. Ellen asks "What does 2130 want from us now?" It is our way of presencing the listening, speaking and actions that are required of us on behalf of those who will be alive in the year 2130. The intended reach and impact of 2130 Partners' work has grown to be 25,000 miles, the world around, and seven generations.

About the Authors:

In addition to their work in 2130 Partners, Suzanne & Dwight Frindt both serve as Chairs (facilitators) of multiple groups for Vistage International, Inc., a worldwide organization with over 14,000 executives who meet regularly in small group interactions and also participate in private coaching sessions. Dwight has been the recipient of numerous annual Vistage Awards and serves as a Best Practice Chair. Suzanne has served on the Chair Advisory Board, facilitated Chair Development workshops and speaks internationally to Vistage groups. Both are ordained Inter-Faith ministers and continue to be long term Investor Activists with The Hunger Project.

Suzanne's clients and audiences view her as a unique fusion of passion and skill, with the ability to hear intention and commitment, support increased leadership and conversational capacities, and facilitate translating intention into reality. She has led programs in such diverse environments as Abu Dhabi, where she was part of the Middle East and North Africa Businesswomen's Summit, Peru training indigenous women leaders, and most recently as a curriculum co-creator and instructor for "The World Academy for the Future of Women" at SIAS International University in China. Suzanne has an MBA from the University of California, Irvine.

Dwight has drawn on both his hands on leadership experience and his background in global non-profit work to develop the leadership philosophy at the heart of his work. In addition to over two decades in executive positions in mining, heavy construction, nuclear plant construction management, real estate acquisition and investment management, he has facilitated more than 1,000 days of leadership workshops and logged more than 13,000 hours of executive coaching. Dwight has an MBA from Harvard University.

How to Reach Us – For More Support

The Operating Principles and the essential notions in this book are fully integrated into all of 2130's work with clients whether in the form of workshops, one-to-one coaching, strategic intensives and other curriculum. To learn more about 2130 Partners and our programs, please visit our website, read our blog, subscribe to it, send it to your friends, become a fan on Facebook, watch our You Tube clips, or connect with us and our work in any way that calls to you!

✓To find out more about Dwight and Suzanne Frindt, or 2130 Partners' latest programs, please go to our web site at http://www.2130partners.com

✓If you would like to get in touch with us the contact page on the web site has information about the best ways to reach us.

✓Our most current writings on leadership can be found on our blog http://www.2130partners.com/blog/

✓Please join our community on our Facebook page http://www.facebook.com/2130partners

✓Video clips about some of our key principles and ideas can be seen on our YouTube channel http://www.youtube.com/2130PartnersLLC

Made in the USA
Charleston, SC
08 July 2011